Lawrence of Arabia

the life, the legend

Lawrence of Arabia

MALCOLM BROWN

the life, the legend

Thames & Hudson

© 2005 Malcolm Brown
Published in association with the Imperial War Museum, London.
www.iwm.org.uk

First published in 2005 in hardcover in the United States of America by
Thames & Hudson Inc., 500 Fifth Avenue, New York, New York 10110

thamesandhudsonusa.com

Library of Congress Catalog Card Number 2005900274

ISBN-13: 978-0-500-51238-8
ISBN-10: 0-500-51238-8

Printed in Singapore by CS Graphics Pte Ltd

CONTENTS

All men dream: but not equally. Those who dream by night in the dusty recesses of their minds wake in the day to find that it was vanity: but the dreamers of the day are dangerous men, for they may act their dream with open eyes, to make it possible. This I did.

Introduction

The *Oxford Book of Modern Quotations* includes just three quotations by T. E. Lawrence in its hundreds of crammed pages. One is the title of his world-famous autobiographical work: *Seven Pillars of Wisdom*, a reworking of a text in the Biblical book of Proverbs. The longest quotation is the first stanza of the dedicatory poem which has introduced every one of the millions of copies of his book produced since it first appeared in public print in the year of his death, 1935: itself a riddle that has given rise to almost as much speculation as the identity of the Dark Lady in Shakespeare's sonnets.

> To S.A.
> I loved you, so I drew these tides of men into my hands
> and wrote my will across the sky in stars
> To earn you Freedom, the seven pillared worthy house
> that your eyes might be shining for me
> When we came

Who or what was S.A.? A woman? A man? A country? A concept? Speculation tends to favour the second answer, identifying a young Arab who became Lawrence's aide and companion during his years just before the First World War as an archaeologist in Syria, though as in the case of all the best riddles, it is highly possible that Lawrence deliberately created an 'enigma' code which he wished to remain unbroken. After all, it is the unsolved mysteries that survive and continue to fascinate, otherwise one's carefully constructed deception plan would soon be as dead as yesterday's crossword puzzle.

The third quotation, the first in the dictionary's order of printing, is from his only other original work *The Mint*, written about his early days in the Royal Air Force, so incautious in its vocabulary that, like *Lady Chatterley's Lover* by the other Lawrence, David Herbert as opposed to Thomas Edward, it could not be published in an unexpurgated edition until long after his death. It reads:

Many men would take the death-sentence without a whimper to escape the life-sentence which fate carries in her other hand.

Anyone who could put his hand to a sentiment like that is clearly no ordinary man-in-the-street, but an individualist marching to his own music and who, if there were to be a cliff anywhere in the region, would almost inevitably be found near its edge.

This was a man with, from the start, a towering ambition. He once stated that he wanted to be a general and knighted by the time he was thirty. He almost made it. In the desert war he exercised, through persuasion and example rather than by the direct issuing of orders, some kind of strategic control over the Arab forces to which he was attached. For much of two years – to use a phrase that has recently achieved an impressive currency and seems to fit his case remarkably well – he wore 'the mask of command'. He never became a knight, but at the age of twenty-eight he was created a Companion of the Order of the Bath, a C.B.: that most quaintly English of honours not far below the level of knighthood; indeed there are those who might consider it the more distinguished. And then he discarded all his honours and walked away. The almost general became the humblest of ordinary servicemen. The man who had become the most admired figure to have emerged out of the war became a down-and-out (his own phrase) in a barrack room. If he had been religious he might have entered a monastery. But religion had been forced on him by a demanding and over-zealous mother and he had reacted by becoming a disorientated sceptic on the edge of losing his faith altogether. So he became a kind of lay monk in the nearest modern equivalent he could find to a monastery: the armed forces, not as the high-flying officer he had once been, but at the lowliest rank available – aircraftman in the Royal Air Force, or private in the Army's Tank Corps. This period saw also a descent to the depths mentally, the suicide option looming at times as far from being merely a notional possibility. In effect, this, for T. E. Lawrence, was his personal ground zero.

He succeeded in lifting himself from this pit of despair, managing, especially in the early 1930s, to achieve a healthier balance, even, almost, a kind of happiness – notably during the years when he devoted himself to such practical ends as the development of air-sea rescue power boats for the RAF, a work which produced a not unimportant legacy: the saving of many airmen's lives during the Second World War. But he was also coping with the legacy of guilt inherited from his dealing with the Arabs during the war years, for which he believed he required punishment; his other paramount ambition, to be a great writer, ran out of subjects, and the end of his RAF career – which had virtually provided him with a substitute family, his own family having virtually disintegrated – presented him with a daunting and uncertain future. It is fair comment to say that this was a man for whom a gracious, peaceful old age was the unlikeliest of outcomes.

In this case perhaps it was no bad thing. Accidental death solved at a stroke the problem of what to do with the rest of his life. T. E. Lawrence – forever running away from the name he was born to and by this time wearing the legal alias of T. E. Shaw – died at the age of forty-six from brain damage resulting from a motorcycling accident on a quiet road in the southern English county of Dorset on a bright and windless May morning. He went out to send a telegram inviting a fellow-writer to lunch on the following day, posted a parcel to a former comrade from his early service days, and on the way back to his secluded cottage a mile or so from the post office in the Army camp at Bovington he clipped the rear-wheel of a bicycle belonging to one of two errand boys who were almost certainly doing nothing more extraordinary than enjoying a lazy ride up the hill. His death after almost a week's coma on 19 May 1935 so vexed and challenged an up-and-coming Australian brain surgeon that it could be said to have become over time a powerful argument for the use of crash-helmets.

This and his other minor legacy in the matter of the saving of lives at sea were, however, sideshows, by-products. His most important legacy was the legend that will not go away – and is not only concerned with the by now almost mythic figure of a man on a camel enacting a heroic dream in one of the world's most famous deserts. He is a man who speaks in other ways to the modern human condition, a man of the *Zeitgeist* according to one commentator, to another – in view of the twists and turns of an outstanding mind in its attempt to achieve some kind of equilibrium – 'a prince of our disorder'. There is something curiously attractive about a high achiever who seems to have everything in his hands, then throws it all away, and turns the rest of his life into a kind of quest, even if it was a quest with no clearly defined goal. Like him or loathe him, respect or dismiss him, this man will be around for a long time yet.

THE YEARS OF HOPE AND AMBITION

PART 1

Opposite: 'Mrs Lawrence'

Opposite: 'Mrs Lawrence' with the first four of her sons, possibly taken by the boys' father, a keen amateur photographer. The photograph probably dates from 1895, when the family was living at Langley Lodge, Hampshire, their last place of refuge before they moved to Oxford. The second son, Thomas Edward, born 1888, is seated on the left.

Thomas Edward Lawrence was the second of five illegitimate sons born to a runaway Anglo-Irish landowner and the governess he had hired to look after the four daughters he had legitimately fathered by his wife, herself a member of the Anglo-Irish Ascendancy. The reason for leaving her was, according to the accepted assumptions, that she had fallen prey to an obsessive religious mania, and that he had come to regard his existence in the family seat, a country-house called South Hill in deep countryside north-west of Ireland's capital, Dublin, as intolerable. His name was Thomas Robert Tighe Chapman, he was a product of Britain's most illustrious public school, Eton, and he was the heir to a baronetcy. Though sufficiently dedicated to his inheritance to have studied at an agricultural college, he was a typical representative of his class and time. 'My father was on the large scale,' his most famous son once wrote of him, 'tolerant, experienced, grand, rash, humoursome, skilled to speak and naturally lord-like. He had been thirty five years in the larger life, a spendthrift, a sportsman and a hard rider and drinker.' Gradually this breezy, unchallenging lifestyle became overshadowed by his wife's insistence on a dour regime of extreme religiosity. The arrival of the young governess – herself far from backward in the matter of Christian belief, being, in Lawrence's words, 'brought up in the Isle of Skye by a Bible thinking-Presbyterian' – produced, as events turned out, not a further intensification of religious gloom but the alluring prospect of escape. Whereas Edith, his wife, had, as she grew older and more serious, evidently abjured the pleasures of the flesh, Sarah, the governess, was by nature deeply and consistently passionate and continued to be so over many years. Overcoming any sense of guilt, master and employee became lovers, both being aware from the start that this was no brief, incautious liaison but a far deeper and more permanent relationship. Indeed, having once sinned, Robert and Sarah compounded their moral felony by making adultery not so much a failing as a way of life.

The affair soon resulted in pregnancy, and in 1885 their first son, Montagu Robert, was born in Dublin, where the two had conspired to live incognito until the child was born. They registered him as Chapman, but when the story got out, as it was bound to do sooner or later, they fled, adopting a surname whose origins were, and remain, obscure. Sarah's birth name was, apparently, Junner, but at some point she seems to have used the name 'Lawrence' (possibly the name of her natural father), and this was the alias under which Thomas and Sarah proceeded to carve out their deviant personal pilgrimage, moving from place to place almost like refugees fearful of pursuit. Thus their second son, the future 'Lawrence of Arabia', was born in Wales in 1888, a third son, William George, in 1889 in Scotland, a fourth, Frank Helier, in 1893 in the Channel Islands, and a fifth, Arnold Walter, in 1900 in Oxford, the city in the heart of England, best known for its ancient university, in which they eventually settled. Their wanderlust had begun in 1885; it was eleven years before they arrived in Oxford, where they slipped into the quiet obscurity of a new, burgeoning suburb on its northern outskirts, to some extent at least the product of the sexual liberation that had followed the abolition of the code of celibacy that had applied to the fellows of Oxford's colleges since the Middle Ages.

They could have found no better sanctuary. There was a church – one among an increasing number in Oxford at that time – with whose doctrines of redemption and salvation they could feel comfortably at home ('God hates the sin, but loves the sinner', was one of Sarah's regular mantras throughout her life, suggesting that ultimately all

Above: South Hill in County Westmeath, the Irish mansion where the Lawrence saga began, with the elopement of its owner with the family governess. Lawrence himself never saw the house, nor did he meet any of his half-sisters, none of whom ever married.

Below: The modest house in Tremadoc, North Wales, where T. E. Lawrence was born.

Right: An early photograph of Lawrence, known throughout his childhood and youth as 'Ned'.

Left: The first four sons in a posed studio photograph: Bob, Will, Ned above; Frank below, in baby clothes.

Above: 2 Polstead Road: the house in North Oxford, where the Lawrence family settled in 1900. In the middle of the social scale of the city's new suburb, semi-detached but still stylish: imposing detached villas to the east, modest two-storey working class houses to the west. Photographs taken in the 1960s.

would be forgiven). There was also a recently established school of considerable quality, expressly designed to meet the changing requirements of one of Europe's highest places of the mind, as it moved into a new, more modern dispensation.

Lawrence's troubled background was a matter of great importance to him throughout his life. Illegitimacy was a serious disadvantage, a shameful secret to be hidden away; this really was an area in which the sins of the parents were visited on the children. One reason why he twice changed his name in his later years was that he knew his given one was an invention, a pseudonym to which he had no real claim. There are strong hints that in his last decade he conceived the idea of being renamed Chapman, of being grafted back somehow into the family tree, of reclaiming the aristocratic connections that had been denied him. As for the name 'Lawrence', in time it was to become anathema for him. In 1923, when a private in the Tank Corps serving under a deliberate alias, he wrote to his Oxford mentor and friend, D. G. Hogarth, 'I've finished with the "Lawrence" episode. I don't like what rumour makes of him – not the sort of man I'd like to be!' The popular abridged edition of *Seven Pillars of Wisdom*, published in 1927 under the title *Revolt in the Desert*, was stated as being by 'T. E. Lawrence', the quotation marks, as we can now see, suggesting a deliberate disclaimer. After his death the wife of his American publisher would write of him: 'He asked us to call him T. E., because he said that was the only part of his name which really belonged to him, and people who were fond of him should call him that.'

Yet in his formative years there was no problem in the name; nor was 'T. E.' part of the equation – to his family and fellow schoolboys he was 'Ned'. There was, however, an eccentricity in the personality. Short – in fact the shortest of the five brothers – but with a powerful and muscular frame, he was not a youth to join the crowd, to play team games; a rough and tumble in the school playground perhaps, but not for him the soccer or rugby field or the stylish elegance of cricket. Instead he became addicted to challenges that required grit and endurance, his greatest feat being a solitary bicycle ride southward through France to the shores of the Mediterranean. This was not just a physical ordeal, to see how many kilometres he could achieve in a day (though he could and did boast of his cycling prowess in appropriate

Left: The City of Oxford High School for Boys. Opened in 1881, it was attended by all five Lawrence brothers. Ned was at the school from 1896 to 1907.

No.	NAME OF BOY.	Name of Parent or Guardian.	Occupation.	ADDRESS.	
599	Glanville. Wilfred Banbury	Edwin	Grocer	Wote Street, Basingstoke.	Sept 30/8
600	Godwin. Charles	Frederick William	Farmer	Beaconsfield, Sandford S.Martin, Steeple Aston.	Sept 3/8
601	Lawrence. Montagu Robert	Thomas R	Independent Means	2 Polstead Road. Oxford.	Dec 29/8
602	Lawrence. Thomas Edward	Thomas R	Independent Means	2 Polstead Road, Oxford	Aug 16/8
603	Allen. Hugh Howard	Hugh James	Tailor	136 High Street, Oxford	July 6/8
604	Allen. James Arnold	Hugh James	Tailor	136 High Street, Oxford	Aug 17/8
605	Allen. Ernest Mortimer	Hugh James	Tailor	136 High Street, Oxford	Oct 25/8
606	Brownsill. William Gerald	J E	Banker	The Bank, Woodstock	Sept 19/8
607	Carter. Herbert Theophilus	Frederick	College Servant	47 High Street, Oxford	Dec 11/8
608	Wood. Frederic	Walter	Farmer	Portway Farm, Buckingham	Jan 24/8
609	Whitehead. Victor Frederick	Alfred William	Organist	65 Banbury Road, Oxford	Jan 16/8
610	Andrews. Reginald Holmes	Henry (grandfather) William	Sadler (grandfather) Mechanic	9 S.Margarets Road, Oxford } 33 Hurst Street. Cowley Road. Oxford	Oct 25/8 Sept 6/8
611	Simmons. George Walter				
612	Kerry. Arthur Henry Goold	Arthur Frank	Schoolmaster	Ekaya, Polstead Road. Oxford	July 21/8
613	Chaundy. Theodore William	Sarah	Printseller	49 Broad Street, Oxford	Jan 18/8
614	Muggeridge... Armenag	Norman Hardwicke Smith (Guardian)	Bursar, Mansfield College	9 Chalfont Road, Oxford	June 26/8
615	Davis. Harry James	Ernest J Crombie (Guardian)	Clergyman	55 Southfield Road, Cowley S.John. Oxford	March 3/8
616	Poole. Arthur Wyatt				

Left: The page from the school register (below), showing the entries for the two elder Lawrence brothers, M. R. and T. E. Note that under the heading 'Occupation', which produced a wide mix of professions including farmer, grocer, tailor, college servant, but also banker, schoolmaster, organist and clergyman, their father, named as 'Lawrence, Thomas R.', stood out, being described as of 'Independent Means', an indication that in spite of having abandoned his original family he still received its financial support.

circles); it was an attempt to reach out and touch the classical world that had fired his mind during endless hours of intensive reading. From here, writing home, he expressed a kind of creed that would dominate much of his life:

...I felt that at last I had reached the way to the South, and all the glorious East; Greece, Carthage, Egypt, Tyre, Syria, Italy, Spain, Sicily, Crete... they were all there, and all within reach... of me. I fancy I know now better than Keats what Cortes felt like, silent upon a peak in Darien. Oh I must get down here, – further out – again! Really this getting to the sea has almost overturned my mental balance: I would accept a passage for Greece tomorrow...

'Further out!' It was a powerful slogan, but far from being mere rhetoric. The medieval as well as the classical world excited him, and in particular he pursued castles, whether near at hand (Caerphilly and Chepstow were high in his list of admirations), or across France, a

Left: A school group of 1906, photographed in the school playground: Ned, eyes firmly fixed on the camera, stands in the centre of the back row.

Below: One of Ned's brass rubbings: the splendid figure of Lord Berkeley, which he found in the parish church of Wootton-under-Edge, Gloucestershire.

'You know, I think, the joy of getting into a strange country in a book: at home when I have shut my door and the town is in bed – and I know that nothing, not even the dawn – can disturb me in my curtains: only the slow crumbling of the coals in the fire: they get so red and throw such splendid glimmerings on the head of Hypnos and the brass-work. And it is lovely too, after you have been wandering for hours in the forest with Percivale or Sagramors le desirous, to open the door, and from over the Cherwell to look at the sun glowering through the valley-mists. Why does one not like things if there are other people about? Why cannot one make one's books live except in the night, after hours of straining? And you know they have to be your own books too, and you have to read them more than once.

...but if you can get the right book at the right time you taste joys – not only bodily, physical, but spiritual also, which pass one out and beyond one's miserable self, as it were through a huge air, following the light of another man's thought. And you can never be quite the old self again.'

From a letter to his mother from France, September 1910

prime favourite being Richard the Lionheart's masterpiece, Château Gaillard, constructed on high ground overlooking the Seine at Les Andelys in Normandy. A fascination with the Crusades, in which Richard was a leading protagonist, was an inevitable corollary of all this. Thus following his move from school to university in 1907 to read history at Jesus College, when required to prepare a thesis for his final examination he offered as its subject a comparison between the castles of western Europe and the Crusader castles of the Middle East, boldly proposing a revisionist view reversing the standard assumption that Europe had led the way in the matter of architectural style. To him the truth was precisely the other way round and the palm should be given to the Crusaders. He devoted the long vacation of 1909 to the necessary field research in Syria and Palestine, undertaking a three-month journey of 1,100 miles visiting as many as thirty-seven castles, much of the time spent going native, almost at one point falling victim to a lunatic gunman (there were even reports of his murder in a regional newspaper). 'Here I am Arab in habits', he wrote in a letter home; 'I will have such difficulty in becoming English again.' It was a prophetic statement. He arrived back in Oxford so thin and gaunt as to be almost unrecognizable, but with the evidence that would guarantee that the thesis to which he would now turn his hand would win him an outstanding degree. He was duly awarded first-class honours in the summer of 1910. No other outcome was possible; he knew more about the subject than his examiners. His findings have long been superseded, but his thesis is still seen as a significant and impressive pioneer work.

In his teens he had made himself well known at Oxford's Ashmolean Museum, by donating archaeological finds unearthed by himself and a school-friend during excavations in the city prior to a spate of rebuilding. The Museum's new Keeper from 1909, D. G. Hogarth, now offered him an opportunity he could not, nor wanted to, resist. He contrived to procure for the young graduate a senior scholarship (formally a Senior Demyship) at his own college, Magdalen, one of Oxford's finest and most prestigious institutions, in order to support him as an assistant to an archaeological dig in the Middle East of which he, Hogarth, was in charge on behalf of the British Museum. The dig was at Carchemish, an ancient Hittite city on the banks of the Euphrates in Syria, where work was about to restart after a considerable interval.

Above: Jesus College, where Lawrence rapidly won the reputation of an unfashionable eccentric.

Below: Lawrence's sketch of the castle of Sahyun, Syria; used as an illustration in his Oxford thesis, later published as *Crusader Castles*.

'The Château Gaillard was so magnificent, and the postcards so abominable, that I stopped there an extra day, and did nothing but photograph, from 6 a.m. to 7 p.m.... its plan is marvellous, the execution wonderful, and the situation perfect. The whole construction bears the unmistakable stamp of genius. Richard I must have been a far greater man than we usually consider him: he must have been a great strategist and a great engineer, as well as a great man-at-arms.'

From a letter to his mother, 11 August 1907

Below: Château Gaillard was not only 'magnificent' in itself, it was a potent link between Europe and the East. Photograph and sketches by Lawrence.

CHEMIN DE RONDE

CHATEAU GAILLARD.

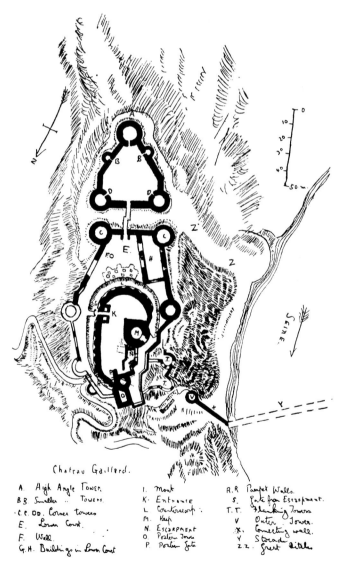

Château Gaillard.

A. High Angle Tower.	I. Moat
B.B. Smaller .. Towers.	K. Entrance
C.C. DD. Corner towers	L. Counterscarp.
E. Lower Court.	M. Keep
F. Wall.	N. Escarpment
G.H. Buildings in Lower Court	O. Postern Tower
	P. Postern Gate

R.R Parapet Walls.
S. Gate from Escarpment.
T.T. Flanking Towers
V. Outer Tower.
X. Connecting wall.
Y. Stockade
ZZ. Great Ditches

So Lawrence went east again, leaving England in early December 1910. As well as working on pottery, he was expedition photographer and organizer of the workforce, a task he took to with a typical energy, and an equally typical eccentricity. At a time when it would have been almost axiomatic to play the imperial white man in charge of the natives, he became their comrade, interpreting his supervisory role in a way that appealed to their natural high spirits. Thus the finding of treasures was celebrated by the firing of pistols; the better the find, the greater number of shots. It was almost as if he were preparing himself, unintentionally, for the companionship of the ranks. He would be the better attuned for his later service in the Royal Air Force and the army because of his easy relationships with his workmen at Carchemish. But before the years in the ranks there would be the more important phase of the desert war, and for that too he was being prepared: by improving his knowledge of the language, not only its structure and literary basis but also its patois and its slang; by acquiring techniques of persuasion and encouragement that would be invaluable during the coming campaigns; and by acquiring a capacity of endurance in the testing circumstances of the East that would make him legendary. His time off was not spent in easy relaxation. In 1911, for example, he embarked on a further long journey in search of more castles and more physical challenge, recording the experience in a memorable diary and another substantial crop of photographs.

He would look back on his Carchemish period as perhaps his happiest. After years of striving and endeavour he could relax: he had time, he wrote, 'to sit down and think, and it is so precious a discovery'. Here too he met the young Arab, nicknamed Dahoum ('the dark one'), whose more formal name was, some sources suggest, Selim Ahmed: possibly the 'S.A.' of the dedicatory poem of *Seven Pillars of Wisdom*. He saw promise in him, trained him in photography, and made him an aide and a companion. In a letter home he described him as 'an interesting character', stating, notably, that he 'altogether has more intelligence than the rank and file'. Suggestions that this might have been a homosexual relationship were vigorously dismissed by the distinguished archaeologist to whom Hogarth handed over the running of the Carchemish excavations in 1912: Leonard, later Sir Leonard Woolley, to become especially famous for his excavations at Ur of the Chaldees.

An archaeologist in the making: a 15th-century beaker (**above**) and 14th-century Baluster jug (**below**), found during excavations in Cornmarket Street, Oxford, presented by Ned Lawrence and his schoolfriend, C. F. C. Beeson, to the Ashmolean Museum.

Above left and right:
Two sheets of illustrations showing pottery excavated at Carchemish. Drawings by R. Campbell Thompson, briefly the deputy leader of the British Museum's team, with autograph notes by Lawrence, dating from 1911.

Right: One of the expedition's notebooks, showing Lawrence's drawings of the inscriptions of an important find in 1911, the Yusuf Beg stone.

Almost certainly the earliest picture of Lawrence in Arab clothes, those of his Arab friend Dahoum, restored to his own garments in the photograph opposite, with the addition (presumably for humorous effect) of a revolver. Photographs by the two sitters, probably 1912.

Many people have found these two parallel pictures puzzling, but it is far more likely that they represent a light-hearted diversion rather than any deviancy. His colleague Leonard Woolley knew Lawrence liked to shock, but he would have firmly refuted any homosexual interpretation. It should also be noted that when he went on his Middle Eastern journeys, Lawrence sometimes wore Arab clothes.

Left: The doorway to the archaeologists' living quarters at Carchemish, featuring the expedition's cook, Haj Wahid, almost certainly acting as scale to show the dimensions of the carving above the door, made by Lawrence in 1912 between digging seasons. He wrote to his family: 'As I had no chisels, I carved it with a screw-driver and a knife. It is a Hittite design and use, and looks very fitting.' The fact that visitors were allowed to assume, and sometimes did, that it was a genuine Hittite carving was a source of much amusement. See also page 192.

Opposite, below: Captain Stewart Newcombe, Royal Engineers, was in charge of the Sinai Survey undertaken in early 1914. Newcombe later served with Lawrence in the desert war, during which this photograph was taken, almost certainly by Lawrence himself. By this time, Newcombe had been promoted to the rank of Lieutenant Colonel.

Above: Lawrence's archaeological camera, specially made for him in 1910. The five lenses include a wide angle and a telephoto. Now in the possession of the Museum of Science, Oxford.

Dahoum was not his only close friend among the workforce. In 1913 Lawrence took Dahoum and the foreman Sheikh Hamoudi on a holiday trip to Oxford, where they briefly became part of the Lawrence household in Polstead Road, the garden sanctuary providing convenient and appropriate accommodation. Riding on girls' bicycles on account of their flowing robes, they seem to have caused little stir in a university town not unused to visitors from afar.

If there were clouds at this period, they related largely to the prospects of war. That illustrious imperial figure Lord Kitchener, who would become Secretary of State for War in 1914 but was at this time British Agent and Consul-General in Egypt, became concerned that in the event of hostilities in the Middle East the Ottoman Empire – or, in the more usual parlance at the time, Turkey – would almost certainly side with Britain's enemies and might threaten that vital lifeline, the Suez Canal. Seeing the Sinai Peninsula as an especially significant area of Turkish-held territory, he ordered that a military survey should be undertaken there, to be carried out by a trusted, experienced officer of the Royal Engineers, Captain Stewart Newcombe. However, the survey needed a civilian cover to allay any Turkish suspicions, and so Woolley and Lawrence, not too far off in Carchemish, were invited, doubtless with a touch of patriotic persuasion, to provide this. Lawrence's version of the task assigned to them was that they were to be 'red herrings, to give archaeological colour to a political job'.

The expedition – which also included Dahoum, partly as helper and servant, but also because he would be especially valuable as 'scale' during photography of the numerous sites they planned to visit – went ahead in early 1914. Although devised for other than scholarly reasons this was no empty or futile task. It was carried out with the support and sponsorship of the Palestine Exploration Fund, for which organization Woolley and Lawrence were mandated to write an account of their findings that would be fit for publication. They returned briefly to Carchemish, but that year's season was a deliberately brief one and in May they closed down the site to return home. They were in England working on their treatise, to be assigned the striking title of *The Wilderness of Zin*, when in August the prospect of international conflict moved from threat to certainty and the First World War began.

Opposite: Lawrence and Woolley (centre, looking to his left), photographed with the expedition work force, 1913. Next to Woolley, left to right, are: the site observer for the Imperial Ottoman Museum, Fuad Bey (an indication that this was a site in Turkish-held territory), the chief local foreman, Sheikh Hamoudi, and (engaging the photographer with a broad smile) Dahoum.

Right: Lawrence and Woolley, standing next to a Hittite slab excavated at the site, with, foreground, a section of the dig's light railway: photograph taken by a visiting German photographer, Heinrich Franke, in 1913.

What were Lawrence's ambitions at this stage of his career? He had a wide range of them, including the desire to produce beautifully designed and finely printed books, even, an idea soon discarded, the urge to become a novelist. But he would later admit to far grander ambitions, even making, in the final page of his best-known book, the remarkable claim that 'I had dreamed, at the City School in Oxford, of hustling into form, while I lived, the new Asia which time was inexorably bringing upon us.' At a more modest level, he had tinkered with what we would now call 'travel writing', if with a serious, historian's purpose. He had started a book on seven eastern cities, but, dissatisfied with it, burned the manuscript sometime in 1914. He had devised a title for it, however, which pleased him sufficiently for him to put it by for possible future use. That title was *Seven Pillars of Wisdom*.

Left: Fareedeh el Akle, the Christian Syrian-born teacher who first instructed Lawrence in Arabic and became a life-long admirer and friend of her precocious pupil.

Above: Dahoum fulfilling the valuable function of acting as scale in one of Lawrence's many archaeological photographs.

Right: The Treasury in the ancient Nabataean city of Petra, carved out of the living rock and one of the supreme wonders of the ancient East. The opportunity to visit Petra, known to generations of travellers as 'a rose-red city, half as old as time' (thanks to the inspired words of an otherwise obscure Victorian cleric, John William Burgon), was for Lawrence a major bonus of the Sinai expedition.

Bab-Es Siq, Petra, by David Bomberg, a Western Front war artist during the 1914–18 war. Painted in 1924 during a tour organized by Sir Ronald Storrs, at that time Governor of Jerusalem and Judea.

Petra – 'the most wonderful place in the world, not for the sake of its ruins, which are quite a secondary affair, but for the colour of its rocks, all red and black and grey with streaks of green and blue, in little wriggly lines…and for the shape of its cliffs and crags and pinnacles, and for the wonderful gorge it has, always running deep in spring-water, full of oleanders, and ivy and ferns, and only just wide enough for a camel at a time, and a couple of miles long. But I have read hosts of most beautifully written accounts of it, and they give one no idea of it at all…and I am sure I cannot write nearly as nicely as they have… so you will never know what Petra is like, unless you come out here…. Only be assured that till you have seen it you have not had the glimmering of an idea how beautiful a place can be.'

Letter from T. E. Lawrence to E. T. Leeds, 28 February 1914

THE YEARS OF TRIUMPH AND TRAUMA

PART 2

Lawrence's war began quietly. While countless others rushed to enlist, he and Woolley continued at maximum speed with the writing of *The Wilderness of Zin*. The work completed, Woolley obtained a commission in the Royal Artillery while Lawrence was enrolled by the geographical division of Military Intelligence in the War Office in London. First employed as a civilian, by late October he had become a second lieutenant on the Special List: i.e. an officer without regimental affiliation. He would remain 'unattached' throughout the war, while rising ultimately to the rank – distinctly unusual for a 'Hostilities Only' officer – of Lieutenant Colonel. For a man supremely unfitted for the camaraderie of an officers' mess, this was a role that fitted his personality perfectly.

His brothers took more conventional routes. Bob, as the eldest son was always known, became a doctor in the Royal Army Medical Corps, Will joined the Royal Flying Corps and Frank joined the infantry. All three served in that crucial arena in north-west Europe which would come to dominate the popular imagination as the supreme symbol of modern, attritional warfare: the Western Front. Within a year Will and Frank were dead: Will was shot down on his first sortie; Frank was killed by a shell when leading his men forward in preparation for an attack. Will, who

Lawrence in his white Arab robes at Akaba, 1917

had served as an observer, was buried with his pilot; his grave can be found in a military cemetery near Cambrai. Frank's fate, as was the case of countless thousands in that war, was to be pronounced as 'missing'; he thus became a member of that huge legion of the lost whose names appear on one of the Western Front's numerous memorials, not in his case the great Arch at Thiepval or the Menin Gate, but a minor shrine at a village called Le Touret, not far from such better-known places as Neuve Chapelle or Béthune.

As for T. E. – the youngest son Arnold, or 'Arnie', as he was generally known, was a mere lad at this time, and therefore not involved – he soon found himself heading east again. Before the year was out he was in Cairo, as part of a hurriedly assembled cadre of the wise and the good whose function was to find out what the Turks were up to in the Middle East (they had indeed come into the war on the side of Britain's enemies, Germany and Austria-Hungary), and to devise ways and means of outwitting them. This was vital work, but it was far from any firing line. Lawrence had made himself over many years a serious student of warfare, but this was war with the pen, the typewriter, the map and the across-table argument, a pallid kind of war of which he would ultimately grow weary.

This phase lasted for almost two years, prompting him to such remarks as 'I am going to be in Cairo till I die', or, 'One would be much happier, I think, in a trench, where one didn't have to worry about politics and informations [sic] all day.' Yet his mind was bubbling with ideas, the most significant of which he encapsulated in a letter to Hogarth written as early as March 1915. Inevitably the Turkish-dominated territories of the Middle East, in particular the Arab tribal areas immediately adjacent to Egypt and the Sudan, were of especial interest to the intelligence gatherers wracking their brains in Cairo. Something had to be done to harness the simmering restlessness in these areas to the central Allied purpose (to aid which a massive expeditionary force was now being assembled in Egypt) of defeating the Turks in battle and sending them packing. Looking at the confused state of Arabian politics, with various tribal leaders pursuing their own conflicting objectives, Lawrence stated in a ringing sentence: 'I want to pull them all together, and to roll up Syria by way of the Hedjaz in the name of the Sherif.' The Sherif was the Grand Sherif Hussein of Mecca, who would indeed fifteen months later launch

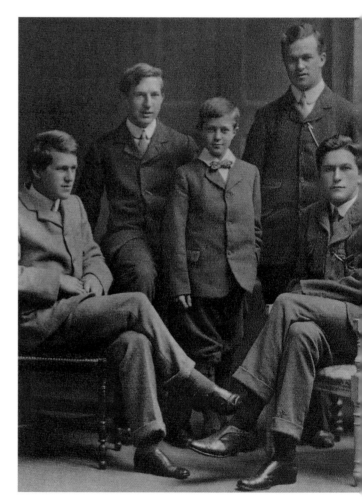

Above: With hindsight, a poignant image, the last known photograph of the five Lawrence brothers together, taken in 1910. Left to right: T. E., Frank, Arnold, Bob, Will.

'I want to pull them all together, and to roll up Syria by way of the Hedjaz in the name of the Sherif.'

Right: T. E. Lawrence in khaki. The photograph was taken later in the war, since it shows him as a Lieutenant-Colonel, but successfully conveys the impression that, at this stage of his career at least, he did not look his best in military uniform, nor did he make any effort to do so. His mind was focused on his ideas, not on the rituals of Army life.

the legendary initiative that would become known as the Arab Revolt, and which ultimately would make Lawrence's name. The Hedjaz (or Hejaz) was that great zone of desert east of the Red Sea where the Revolt would take hold. Damascus, too, was a vital part of Lawrence's concept, as was his suspicion of French ambitions in this quarter, ambitions which he intended by hook or by crook to thwart. To him the French were almost as much an enemy as the Turks. If events turned out as he hoped, he wrote, 'we can rush right up to Damascus, and biff the French out of all hope of Syria. It's a big game, and at last one worth playing.' In effect, he was laying down the scenario of events to come with a quite amazing perspicacity. David Garnett, subsequently editor of the first comprehensive collection of Lawrence's letters, called this 'probably the most remarkable document Lawrence ever wrote. It shows that he had already planned the campaign which he was to carry to a victorious conclusion three years later.'

The 'big game' he hoped for began in earnest in June 1916. Sherif Hussein, emboldened by the promise of British and French support, threw down the gauntlet to the Turks. The task of challenging the enemy was assigned to his sons, Ali, Abdullah, Feisal and Zeid, who took to the field each with his own small force to do battle. But spontaneity and enthusiasm could not compensate for a lack of an overall strategy, and it was the fact that after three months the Revolt was producing few tangible results that brought Lawrence to Arabia.

He went there in October 1916; he would return home in October 1918. These were the two years that made him, but they were also the years that, effectively, implanted the cultural and psychological virus that almost destroyed him. As with the war itself, his Arabian adventure began undramatically. He sailed down the Red Sea to Jidda with a senior member of the British administration in Egypt, Ronald, later Sir Ronald Storrs, where he found himself the third man of a small British delegation seeking to find ways of re-energizing the new revolutionary movement, the other party involved being the British Resident in Jidda, Colonel C. E. Wilson. He was observer and note-taker rather than participant, though still capable of astounding the man they had come to see, Abdullah, the Sherif's second son, with his detailed knowledge when his opinion was invoked or spontaneously offered. Having arrived in Jidda on the 16th, on the 19th he and Storrs sailed north to Rabegh,

Grand Sherif Hussein, Emir of Mecca, founder and figurehead of the Arab Revolt; photograph by the Staff Surgeon of HMS *Dufferin,* dated 12 December 1916.

where they met the Sherif's eldest son, Ali. His career really began when, with crucial help from Storrs, he gained permission to visit the third son, Feisal, who was encamped a hundred miles inland, rather nearer to the enemy than the forces of Ali or Abdullah, in Wadi Safra. Thus he came to embark on the first of his countless desert journeys, itself no easy one being undertaken at speed with only brief respites. He was now on his own, not as a plenipotentiary but with the opportunity to make himself one. Literally almost overnight, he mutated from a junior aide, virtually an intelligence sidekick, to a delegate with a vital mission, namely that of discovering to which Arab leader would seem the likeliest to bring the revolt to success. The authorities in Cairo needed to know what kind of help would be effective and where. Implicitly the criterion was not precedence in status or seniority but in practicality and promise. Thus it came about that the leader given precedence was the third son, Feisal. A remarkable confrontation took place in Feisal's camp in Wadi Safra, and from that meeting emerged the two figures who, to a substantial extent, would occupy the centre stage of the Arab Revolt from now forward. There are divergent views, but it is arguably not far wrong to see these two principals as Feisal the flame and Lawrence the brain, in effect the double mainspring of the burgeoning new movement.

Lawrence's recommendations were accepted, and immediately backed with the promise of money and arms. It was all but inevitable that the flame and the brain (though no one would have seen the situation in those terms) would be united. Before many weeks were out he had left his Cairo desk job for good, and was officially appointed as Feisal's adviser in the Hejaz. At the latter's request, khaki soon gave way to Arab dress; Feisal did not want a European officer in conspicuous military uniform about his camp and Lawrence, who had occasionally donned native dress during his time in Syria, was only too happy to oblige. In any case, Arab clothes were, as he delicately put it, 'cleaner and more decent in the desert', offering an opportunity for personal privacy, not to mention coolness and comfort, which a conventional army uniform could not. He had never cut much of a figure as a soldier; indeed he had inspired some of the senior regulars around him with an almost overpowering urge to order him to polish his buttons, get his hair cut and learn how to salute his superiors rather than amble up to them with his hands in his pockets. In Arab clothes he was transformed. They masked his short stature, gave a dramatic frame to his strong features and his (by all accounts) magnetic eyes, helping him to achieve a presence and a style which not only disarmed his previous critics but also greatly impressed his new comrades in war.

Superficially at least, he took the change of scene and costume lightly. There was no overt hint of manifest destiny. He would later state that he was sent back to Arabia 'much against [his] will', but in December 1916 he wrote to the officer in charge of the Arab Bureau, the recently formed intelligence organization dedicated to the Arab Revolt to which he was now formally attached, that he wanted to 'rub off his British habits and go off with Feisal for a bit', adding: 'Amusing job and all new country'. The country was new, but overall the job – as he doubtless sensed in his innermost self – would prove itself far from amusing

It is important to define his role in the campaigns that followed. He would often be referred to after the war as the man who led the Arabs to victory. Later, in correspondence with military thinkers such as Liddell Hart, he would discuss his role in terms of generalship. But this was essentially a reference to the matter of strategy and tactics, not to actual command. For a striking analysis of his wartime role there could be no better comment than that of one of those regular officers who initially deplored his appearance but later came to admire his perspicacity, his wisdom and his touch with the tribes, Colonel Pierce Joyce. Though senior in rank, Joyce saw that when Lawrence was in conference with the Arab tribal leaders he was the crucial figure; recognizing this, the Colonel deferred to the young Captain. At such conferences, wrote Joyce, 'Lawrence rarely spoke. He merely studied the men around him and when the arguments ended as they usually did, in smoke, he then dictated his plan of action which was usually adopted and everyone went away satisfied. It was not, as is often supposed, by his individual leadership of hordes of Bedouin that he achieved success in his daring ventures, but by the wise selection of tribal leaders and by providing the essential grist to the mill in the shape of golden rewards for work well done.'

Joyce's mention of gold adds an important element to the story. Leaders might fight for a political goal, but irregulars such as the Bedouin tribesmen who largely provided the driving force of the Revolt fought for cash. Lawrence understood this perfectly and played to this predilection. Writing to his friend and literary adviser Edward Garnett in 1927, he told

Above: Emir Abdullah, second son of the Grand Sherif; pastel portrait by Eric Kennington, 1921. Not at first admired by Lawrence, but later an important figure in the Middle East until his assassination in 1951

Right: Emir Feisal, third son, and leader of the main thrust of the Arab Revolt. Portrait by Augustus John painted during the Paris Peace Conference in 1919: chosen by Lawrence as frontispiece to the subscribers' edition of *Seven Pillars of Wisdom*, 1926.

'*...almost regal in appearance.... Far more imposing personally than any of his brothers. Looks very like the monument of Richard I at Fontevraud.... A popular idol, and ambitious; full of dreams and the capacity to realise them.*'

Lawrence's account of meeting Emir Feisal for the first time at Hamra, 23 October 1916

Left: Lawrence, for once looking ill at ease in Arab robes, circa February 1917, by an unknown photographer.

'Suddenly Feisal asked me if I would wear Arab clothes like his own when in the camp.... Besides, the tribesmen would then understand how to take me... they would behave towards me as though I were really one of the leaders;... I agreed at once, very gladly.... And the Arab things were cleaner and more decent in the desert.'

Above: Bodyguard to the Emir Feisal, portrayed by the official war artist James McBey, who described him as 'a gigantic Abyssinian negro, his kit consisting of weapons of all epochs, from the Semitic scimitar to the latest Mauser automatic'.

him: 'When an Arab did something individual and intelligent during the war I would call him to me, and opening a bag of sovereigns would say, "Put in your hand", and this was thought the very height of splendour. Yet it was never more than £120: but the exercise of spreading and burying your fingers in gold made it feel better than a cold-blooded counting out of two or three hundred pounds.'

Lawrence's essential gift to the Revolt was, in fact, almost a denial of generalship; in other words, he devised an overall strategic plan that promoted the concept of a war *without* battle, avoiding head-to-head encounters, and thus not incurring the heavy casualty counts of normal warfare, which he saw as unnecessary. It was more important to outwit the enemy than to kill him. Thus there was no wisdom in confronting an army such as that of the Ottoman Empire which with its superior fire-power and its fully trained fighting force would easily massacre an ad hoc guerrilla force attempting a headlong attack. Go for the enemy's *matériel*, not his men. 'The death of a Turkish bridge or rail, machine or gun or charge of high explosive,' he wrote, 'was more profitable to us than the death of a Turk.' In all this, he was building on an existing Bedouin strength; this was their natural style of warfare. But the desire to avoid bloodshed as a principle was his own. To the culture of a war infamous for its huge casualty lists Lawrence added a moving concept of his own: that of the 'rings of sorrow' that widen out from any individual, unnecessary death. He would not always be able to stick to his rules. There would inevitably be casualties, sometimes on a large scale. He would have his own moments of blood-lust. But from a time when lives, civilian as well as military, were increasingly seen as expendable, his quietly expressed philosophy emerges as a still small voice of protest.

The bonding of Feisal and Lawrence was not just a matter of compatible personalities. They shared similar ambitions for the Revolt's further development. Damascus was an essential part of Lawrence's plan as outlined to Hogarth in his letter of 1915. Feisal was of the same mind. Thus the whole impetus of the campaign as the year 1917 began was to move north out of the Hejaz and towards Syria, of which Damascus was the capital. As much as wanting his own side to win, he wanted the Arabs to perform so well that it would give them a claim to freedom. He cared more for the fate of the Arabs in the post-war world to come than he did

Left: The quay at the port of Yenbo.

Below: The house occupied by Lawrence in Yenbo, winter 1916. Both photographs by Lawrence.

for the British. They could look after themselves. The Arabs needed all the help and encouragement they could get.

Feisal's force paused for a time in Yenbo, where Lawrence briefly went into winter quarters; then in January 1917 it headed north to seize another Red Sea port, Wejh. This was not an open town ripe for possession, but an occupied one with a small but significant Turkish garrison. An attack was planned in co-operation with the Royal Navy, but Feisal's army moved more slowly than anticipated, arriving to find the port already taken. There had been brief but fierce fighting, leaving twenty dead and a British seaplane pilot fatally wounded while undertaking an aerial reconnaissance. Lawrence was furious; a few days' patient siege would have brought the same result without the smashing and the killing, which he described as 'wanton'.

Taking Wejh was a major gain, giving the Arabs a strong base from which to attack the Hejaz Railway and proving Feisal an effective leader. To his camp now came the veteran chief of the Howeitat tribe, Auda Abu Tayi. To the scholarly young Englishman he seemed like a warrior out of medieval romance, a knight-errant, almost a Wagnerian Siegfried. 'He sees life as a saga', he wrote of him. 'All events in it are significant and all personages heroic. His mind is packed (and generally overflows) with stories of old raids and epic poems of fights.'

The present tense in this statement is highly significant. This was not written years later, in peaceful circumstances and admiring retrospect. It was written *at the time*, and duly despatched to Cairo for printing in the *Arab Bulletin*, the confidential digest of the findings of the Arab Bureau. Were ever such florid despatches written in modern war?

The War in the Desert: The Opening Phase

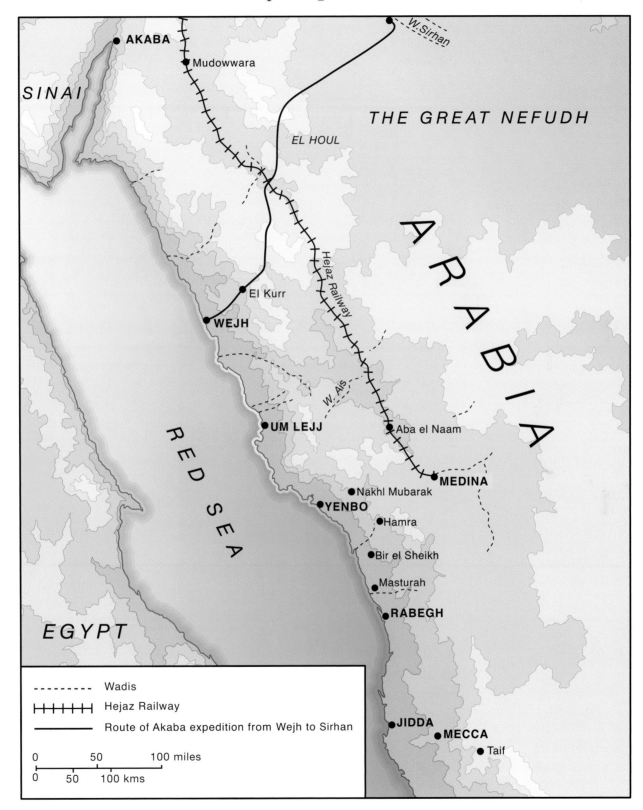

'He sees life as a saga. All events in it are significant and all personages heroic.'

Probably not, but this is where the story assumes the flavour of the novel, which almost inevitably has to rely on seemingly unlikely coincidences. For who was the editor in Cairo who set the standard by which the reports of the various officers scattered about the Arabian peninsula were judged? None other than Lawrence's former mentor, D. G. Hogarth, now wearing the uniform of a Lieutenant Commander of the Royal Navy and a senior figure in British intelligence. Hogarth's firm belief, expressly stated in relation to the *Arab Bulletin*, was that 'it was as easy to write in decent English as in bad, and much more agreeable'. The result was that the *Bulletin* had 'from the first a literary tinge not always present in Intelligence Summaries'. It has been long claimed by such authors as the American Paul Fussell, that the war of the Western Front was a literary war. The same could be stated of the Arabian campaign, and here the undoubted star was T. E. Lawrence, though there were not a few other contributors of distinction, such as Storrs, Newcombe, Hogarth himself (though his duties often took him elsewhere), and, later, the redoubtable traveller, H. St. John Philby.

Auda came to Feisal's camp because he was from a tribe some way to the north and wanted to find out why the Revolt was not purposefully moving in his direction. His impatience and his obvious energy were clearly key factors in inspiring the next, arguably the most dramatic gesture of the whole Revolt: the bid to take Akaba.

Akaba was at the northern end of the Red Sea, a Turkish-held garrison which by all the normal rules of war cried out to be attacked from the sea and from the south. The idea of taking it from inland had been discussed in high circles in Cairo back in the summer of 1916, but had been thought too high-risk for conventional forces. Now, with Auda's support, it seemed feasible. There has been serious, and thoughtful, debate as to who came up with this dazzlingly simple concept. It was a natural initiative to the Arabs, says one school of thought; yet it was Lawrencian through and through, says another. Whatever its origin, it was a stroke of genius.

Such an attack could not be mounted overnight. It would take time, and much careful and judicious persuasion to recruit men from tribes somewhat nearer to the punitive guns of the Turks to support an initiative of such daring. Under the command of an outstanding Arab leader, Sherif Nasir of Medina, and with Auda and Lawrence as his council of war, an

Left to right: Auda ibn Zaal, Mohammed Abu Tayi (Auda's son), an unidentified member of the Howeitat tribe, Auda Abu Tayi, and Zaal ibn Motlog, Auda's nephew. Photograph by Lawrence, taken in Amman at the same time as the close-up of Auda on page 46.

expeditionary force set out from Wejh in circumstances of scrupulous secrecy, heading out into the desert in a wide loop in order to bear down on Akaba from the landward side. It was an operation of almost classic simplicity – the Japanese would employ the same ruse at Singapore in the Second World War – and it worked brilliantly. On 6 July the expedition reached its goal. The capture of Akaba – in Lawrence's words 'for months... the horizon of our minds, the goal' – has been fairly described as the turning point of the Arab Revolt.

Famously, Lawrence rushed off to Egypt to be first with the good news. And there he met another crucial figure in the story: General Sir Edmund Allenby, newly arrived from France to take a more positive grip on what had come to be known as the Palestine front, and where two failed attempts at routing the Turks had put paid to the career of the previous commander-in-chief, thus creating a vacancy which Allenby now brilliantly filled. Allenby was to become, in effect, Lawrence's second Hogarth.

Seizing Akaba opened up for Feisal's Arabs the opportunity to collaborate, if inevitably in a subsidiary role, with the Egyptian Expeditionary Force, which, energized by its new assertive commander general, was about to change the face of the Middle Eastern war. The big general – his nickname 'The Bull' gives some notion of his personal presence and impact – and the small maverick officer, ushered into the great man's presence in his campaign-soiled Arab robes, took to each other at once, seeing advantage in working together in the campaign to come. 'The nearest to my longings for a master', was Lawrence's verdict on his new patron, a notable accolade from a man well known for his dismissive attitude to the run of professional soldiers. From now forward he was the key liaison officer between Allenby and the Arabs, the latter gaining in respect and importance as they assumed the role of being Allenby's irregular right wing.

This was the tone set for the second stage of the Revolt and for the further stages of the Palestine campaign. It is necessary not to overstate the Arabs' importance or input. When in due time the goal of Damascus was reached, it was Allenby's mighty conventional force advancing first along the Mediterranean coast and then striking inland that won the day and deserved the true glory. The Arabs were useful gadflies to the east, harassing, unsettling and pinpricking the enemy rather like single spies

Above: A toast to Arab success: Jaafar Pasha, a former regular officer of the Turkish Army who had defected to the Arab cause, Emir Feisal, and Colonel Pierce Joyce, in Wadi Kuntilla, August 1917. Joyce was originally dismayed at Lawrence's slovenly appearance in khaki, but later came to admire his sure touch with the Arab leaders.

The War in the Desert: The Final Phase

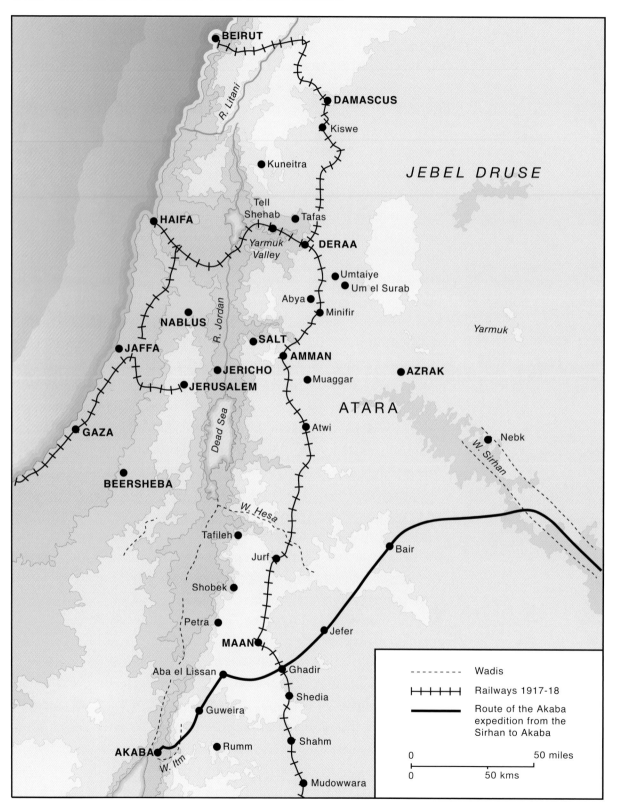

- - - - - - - - -	Wadis
⊢⊢⊢⊢⊢⊢	Railways 1917-18
▬▬▬▬▬	Route of the Akaba expedition from the Sirhan to Akaba

0   50 miles

0   50 kms

while Allenby provided the big battalions. But history is only partly about what actually happened; it is also about how what happened is perceived. There can be no question that the Arabs came out of their war with a high enough profile, and enough genuine actual achievement, to put them on to the international stage for good. They had fought to the best of their abilities, and thanks to them the long umbilical cord of the Hejaz Railway stretching from Medina to Damascus had been in serious disarray for many months. Railway-loving countries such as Britain found great appeal in that. They had, of course, the advantage of having on their side one of the most unusual soldiers, and one of the most successful publicists of modern times, in former Captain, now Colonel T. E. Lawrence.

For him this was a triumph, but the Revolt had also been a time of trauma. He had long known that Allied plans for the redrawing of the Middle Eastern map after the war gave short shrift to the dream of Arab political freedom which had inspired him throughout the campaign, and through which he had inspired others. His great hope was that they would be the better rewarded the better they performed, but when asked by Arabs of distinction and influence about British intentions he found himself having to prevaricate, to emphasize the best of the various pledges that had leaked out of Cairo and play down the worst. A confrontation on these lines with Nuri Shalaan, veteran chief of the Rualla tribe, put him in a very difficult predicament. As he later wrote: 'In his mood, upon my answer, lay the success or failure of Feisal. My advice, uttered with some agony of mind, was to trust the latest in date of the contradictions. This disingenuous answer promoted me, in six months, to be chief confidence man.' He subsequently coined a harsher phrase, describing himself, in relation to the various other British officers involved in one way or another in the campaign, as 'the chief crook of our gang.'

As well as being unavoidably devious on this score, later, following the publication of the Balfour Declaration of November 1917, which stated that the British viewed with favour the establishment of a Jewish national home in Palestine, he was saddled by Cairo with the task, as he defined it himself, of ensuring that 'the Arab attitude shall be sympathetic, for the duration of the war at least'. All this was a tall order for a man under constant pressure, who, when he tried in early 1918 to

Above: A so-called 'tulip' bomb exploding on the Hejaz Railway. In a post-war treatise, Lawrence wrote of the style of demolition used to create this effect: 'the appearance of a piece of rail treated by this method is most beautiful, for the sleepers rise up in all manner of varied forms, like the early buds of tulips'.

give up his role in the desert, was promptly sent back because of his indispensability. So he was compelled to 'resume his mantle of fraud in the East' and returned to his war.

There were highlights. He was present at Allenby's triumphal entry into Jerusalem in December 1917, hurriedly kitted out in uniform, and thereby cutting a distinctly modest figure in the background of the official newsreels. As a student of the Crusades and a man with a Christian, indeed deeply Biblical background, this was an event of immense importance. He would later call it 'the supreme moment of the war.'

There were portents. In Jerusalem he met the American journalist Lowell Thomas, visiting the Middle East at the suggestion of John Buchan in search of a good uplifting war story, not having seen much chance of one in the sterile wastes of the Western Front. Thanks to Sir Ronald Storrs, now the Military Governor of Jerusalem, the two were introduced. In that instance, it could be claimed, the seeds of legend were being sown, for this was the man who would subsequently turn the, at this stage, unknown archaeologist-soldier into 'Lawrence of Arabia'.

There was also the darkest moment of his war: the incident at Deraa in November 1917, when, according to Lawrence's vivid account in *Seven Pillars*, he was savagely beaten by Turkish captors and subjected to the humiliation of male rape, later stating that 'in Deraa that night the citadel of my integrity [was] irrevocably lost.' There have been many claims that this was an invention; an obligatory punishment scene inserted as though into a work of fiction. But there are arguably too many later references in his letters and writings to dismiss this as merely a literary invention. In an early version of *Seven Pillars*, he wrote that that night in Deraa had left him 'maimed, imperfect, only half myself. It could not have been the defilement, for no one held the body in less honour than I did myself. Probably it had been the breaking of the spirit by that frenzied nerve-shattering pain which had degraded me to beast level when it made me grovel to it, and which has journeyed with me ever since, a fascination and terror and morbid desire, lascivious and vicious, perhaps, but like the striving of a moth towards its flame.'

He would never again be the man he was before Deraa.

Plans for 1918 were seriously delayed owing to the massive make-or-break offensives by the Germans in France in the year's early months. With many of Allenby's best troops recalled to France as reinforcements,

The face of a man who has known the highs and lows of war. Pastel portrait of Lawrence by Eric Kennington, included in *Seven Pillars of Wisdom*.

> *'The strongest motive throughout had been a personal one, not mentioned here, but present to me, I think, every hour of these two years. Active pains and joys might fling up, like towers, among my days: but, refluent as air, this hidden urge re-formed, to be the persisting element of life, till near the end. It was dead, before we reached Damascus.'*

it was not until much later in the year than hoped that Allenby's final thrust against the Turks began. Feisal's force aided as best they could, but their advance threw up an episode that presented a challenge to Lawrence, which showed that he too had travelled far since he had elaborated his minimal casualty theories in more innocent days, eighteen months earlier. Advancing north they witnessed the massacre of the people of a village that was home to a tribal chief riding with them, Tallal. Suicidally, Tallal charged his enemies in a frenzy of rage only to fall riddled with Turkish bullets. 'God give him mercy,' cried Auda, 'but we will take his price', and for the first time in his war Lawrence ordered a 'no prisoners' eye-for-an-eye revenge.

Damascus was entered on 1 October 1918. Three days later Lawrence, with Allenby's permission, left to return to England. This might be seen as a premature quitting of the scene at the moment of victory. But for him the end of the campaign had, he would later claim, 'disclosed the exhaustion of [his] main springs of action'; and since it was now becoming increasingly clear that everywhere the war was approaching its end he sensed that the best arena in which to pursue his hopes and ambitions would be in the corridors of power in Europe.

Seven Pillars of Wisdom ends at this point in the story. Its final page, italicized to imply that it is, in effect, a kind of codicil to the narrative pages which precede it, includes this eloquent passage 'The strongest motive throughout had been a personal one, not mentioned here, but present to me, I think, every hour of these two years. Active pains and joys might fling up, like towers, among my days: but, refluent as air, this hidden urge re-formed, to be the persisting element of life, till near the end. It was dead, before we reached Damascus.'

It is known that Dahoum died of typhus, sometime during the war, possibly as early as 1916. But the writer of these carefully crafted sentences was T. E. Lawrence, not one to wear his heart on his sleeve, nor to reveal himself easily to the public or even his closest friends. This, together with the presumably deliberate obfuscation provided by the choice of the pronoun 'it' rather than 'he' – or even 'she' – in the final sentence, suggests that whatever else he was trying to suggest or hint at, the veil was not being twitched away. The mystery remains, as it was doubtless meant to.

'*About that night I shouldn't tell you, because decent men don't talk about such things. For fear of being hurt, or rather to earn five minutes of respite from a pain which drove me mad, I gave away the only possession we are born into the world with – our bodily integrity. It's an unforgivable matter, an irrecoverable position: and it's that which has made me forswear decent living, and the exercise of my not-contemptible wits and talents.*'

Lawrence to Mrs Charlotte Shaw, March 1923,
on his experience at Deraa in 1917.

A Kennington sketch dated 1921, omitted from *Seven Pillars* because its subject found it curiously unnerving.

Feisal's army entering Yenbo

One of a sequence of photographs taken by Lawrence as Feisal's force approached the Red Sea port of Yenbo in December 1916, from the vantage point of the town's Medina Gate.

The beginning: Jidda, October 1916

Jidda from the sea: an image
from the Lowell Thomas Archive

'We had the accustomed calm run to Jidda, in the delightful Red Sea climate, never too hot while the ship was moving. By day we lay in shadow; and for great part of the glorious nights we would tramp up and down the wet decks under the stars in the steaming breath of the southern wind. But when at last we anchored in the outer harbour, off the white town hung between the blazing sky and its reflection in the mirage which swept and rolled over the wide lagoon, then the heat of Arabia came out like a drawn sword and struck us speechless. It was midday; and the noon sun in the East, like moonlight, put to sleep the colours. There were only lights and shadows, the white houses and black gaps of streets: in front, the pallid lustre of the haze shimmering upon the inner harbour: behind, the dazzle of league after league of featureless sand, running up to an edge of low hills, faintly suggested in the far away mist of heat.'

SEVEN PILLARS OF WISDOM

Jidda

Typical street scenes: photographed by Lawrence not in 1916 but in 1921, and included in the subscribers' edition of *Seven Pillars of Wisdom*.

Feisal the Flame

The Emir Feisal, photographed at Wejh, early 1917, acknowledged by Lawrence at their first meeting as the natural leader of the Arab Revolt.

'I felt at first glance that this was the man I had come to Arabia to seek – the leader who would bring the Arab Revolt to full glory. Feisal looked very tall and pillar-like, very slender, in his long white silk robes and his brown head-cloth bound with a brilliant scarlet and gold cord. His eyelids were dropped; and his black beard and colourless face were like a mask against the strange, still watchfulness of his body. His hands were crossed in front of him on his dagger.

I greeted him. He made way for me into the room, and sat down on his carpet near the door. As my eyes grew accustomed to the shade, they saw that the little room held many silent figures, looking at me or at Feisal steadily. He remained staring down at his hands, which were twisting slowly about his dagger. At last he inquired softly how I had found the journey. I spoke of the heat, and he asked how long from Rabegh, commenting that I had ridden fast for the season. "And do you like our place here in Wadi Safra?" "Well; but it is far from Damascus."

The word had fallen like a sword in their midst. There was a quiver. Then everybody present stiffened where he sat, and held his breath for a silent minute. Some, perhaps, were dreaming of far off success: others may have thought it a reflection on their late defeat. Feisal at length lifted his eyes, smiling at me, and said, "Praise be to God, there are Turks nearer us than that".'

SEVEN PILLARS OF WISDOM

'I'm sending you a photograph or two with this letter: none of them are very interesting, but some day we may be glad of them… One of the prints to appear, showing the Sherifian camp at dawn, in Wadi Yenbo, was taken by me at 6 a.m. in January last, and is a very beautiful picture. Most sunrise pictures are taken at sunset, but this one is really a success.'

From a letter to his family, 8 January 1918

The Sherifian camp at dawn

From mid-December 1916 to mid-January 1917 Feisal's force was encamped at Nakhl Mubarak, a date grove close to Yenbo. The pause gave Lawrence the opportunity which he took whenever possible to record on camera the locations and progress of the desert campaign.

The advance to Wejh

Emir Feisal (centre) and Sherif Sharraf leading the Ageyl bodyguard on the first stage of the journey to Wejh, January 1917, as photographed by Lawrence. The angle of the photograph and its closeness to the leaders clearly indicates the young liaison officer's high status in Feisal's force.

'Our start was set for January the eighteenth just after noon… We watched Feisal. He got up from his rug… caught the saddle-pommels in his hands, put his knee on the side… The slave released the camel, which sprang up. When it was on its feet Feisal passed his other leg across its back, swept his skirts and his cloak under him by a wave of the arm, and settled himself in the saddle. As his camel moved we had jumped for ours, and the whole mob rose together, some of the beasts roaring, but the most quiet, as trained she-camels should be…. The camels took their first abrupt steps….'

SEVEN PILLARS OF WISDOM

'*We are no longer Arabs but a People.*'

*Comment of a young tribal leader to Lawrence,
during the journey to Wejh,* SEVEN PILLARS OF WISDOM

Coming into Wejh

A classic Lawrence photograph: Feisal's army approaching Wejh, 25 January 1917.

Feisal's camp at Wejh

Again as photographed by Lawrence, with, inset, Lawrence himself, sporting his Arab robes, though adhering to his normal habit of wearing a wrist watch. Clearly, from the background, the photograph was taken at Wejh, presumably by the person, identity unknown, who took the photograph on page 42.

'As it was the custom in Wejh to camp wide apart, very wide apart, my life was spent in moving back and forth, to Feisal's tents, to the English tents, to the Egyptian Army tents, to the town, the port, the wireless station, tramping all day restlessly up and down those coral paths in sandals or barefoot, hardening my feet, getting by slow degrees the power to walk with little pain over sharp and burning ground, tempering my already trained body for greater endeavour.'

SEVEN PILLARS OF WISDOM

Riding against the enemy

Left: One of Feisal's youngest lieutenants, Sherif Ali ibn el Hussein of the Harith tribe: pastel by Eric Kennington, drawn in 1921, when Ali was twenty-three. Lawrence wrote of him: 'His courage, his resource and his energy were proven. There had never been any adventure, since our beginning, too dangerous for Ali to attempt, nor a disaster too deep for him to face with his high yell of a laugh.... He was physically splendid.... In addition, Ali could outstrip a trotting camel on his bare feet, keep his speed over half a mile and then leap into the saddle.' (*Seven Pillars of Wisdom*). Sherif Ali was an ideal recruit for the style of warfare which was the hallmark of the Arab Revolt.

Opposite: Troops on the march at Bir el Amri, under the command of Sherif Sharref, March 1917.

'...suppose we were (as we might be) an influence, an idea, a thing intangible, invulnerable, without front or back, drifting about like a gas? Armies were like plants, immobile, firm-rooted, nourished through long stems to the head. We might be a vapour, blowing where we listed...

Most wars were wars of contact, both forces striving into touch to avoid tactical surprise. Ours should be a war of detachment. We were to contain the enemy by the silent threat of a vast, unknown desert....'

SEVEN PILLARS OF WISDOM

Sinews of war

The desert campaign could not be won by strategy alone. From the start, there was an urgent need for supplies – the *matériel* with which to fuel and sustain the campaign. Hence the 'shopping list', left, written by Lawrence on the back of an army signals and messages pad, dating from July 1917. Morale was also vital, as was money: hence the reference to 6,000 cigarettes and £16,000 in cash, in addition to such basic elements as ammunition, dynamite and Lewis guns. Coffee cups and thermos flasks also appear in the list, for an army had to drink as well as fight, and coffee was the standard beverage of hospitality in Arabia.

On the edge of achievement

Below: Lawrence photographed by an officer of the Royal Flying Corps, B. E. Leeson (to become a lifelong friend), at Rabegh, just north of Jidda, March 1917.

Right: Lawrence on a camel, photographer unknown, 1917. It can be safely assumed that whoever took this 'snap' had no idea that he was capturing one of the iconic images of the twentieth century.

Akaba: The Crucial Blow

The port of Akaba, photographed after its capture in July 1917. The impression of a somnolent beach resort in the heat of summer belies the fact that this was meant to be a stoutly defended enemy-held port, but the ease with which it fell suggests that this photograph caught its essential mood.

Right: Lawrence's own highly dramatic photograph of the attack on Akaba on 6 July 1917. At a time when photographs from the Western Front in France and Flanders were usually taken on high-quality static cameras, it is remarkable that Lawrence, on his small Kodak using 120 negative film, could achieve action shots that match the images emanating from much later wars. Unlike the photographer referred to on page 74, almost certainly unaware of the significance of the image he had recorded, there is little question that Lawrence realized the importance of this photograph. It was living proof of the effectiveness of his policy of nip and tuck, of using surprise as a weapon of war. Long seen as a striking photograph in itself, it should also be recognized as a vital military document, with a resonance lasting long beyond the time when it was taken.

'For months Akaba had been the horizon of our minds, the goal: we had had no thought, we had refused thought, of anything beside.... Then we raced through a driving sand-storm down to Akaba... and splashed into the sea on July the sixth, just two months after our setting out from Wejh.'

SEVEN PILLARS OF WISDOM

Winning support

Left: General Sir Edmund Allenby, Commander-in-Chief, Egyptian Expeditionary Force, 1917–18. Lawrence's best efforts might have failed if he had not found a commanding general astute enough to harness them to the central Allied purpose: Allenby was that man. Lawrence recognized his calibre at once, while the seizure of Akaba impressed Allenby as to the validity of Lawrence's credentials.

Securing the base

Below and right: These photographs show Akaba being secured as a base for future strikes against the enemy. But the port also needed defence against possible strikes by the enemy; hence the presence, far right, at the so-called Chatham Pier, of HMS *Humber*, a light monitor armed with three six-inch guns, successfully judged to be a sufficiently powerful deterrent.

'Allenby, gigantic and red and merry,
fit representative of the Power which
had thrown a girdle of humour and
strong dealing round the world.'

SEVEN PILLARS OF WISDOM

Akaba in retrospect

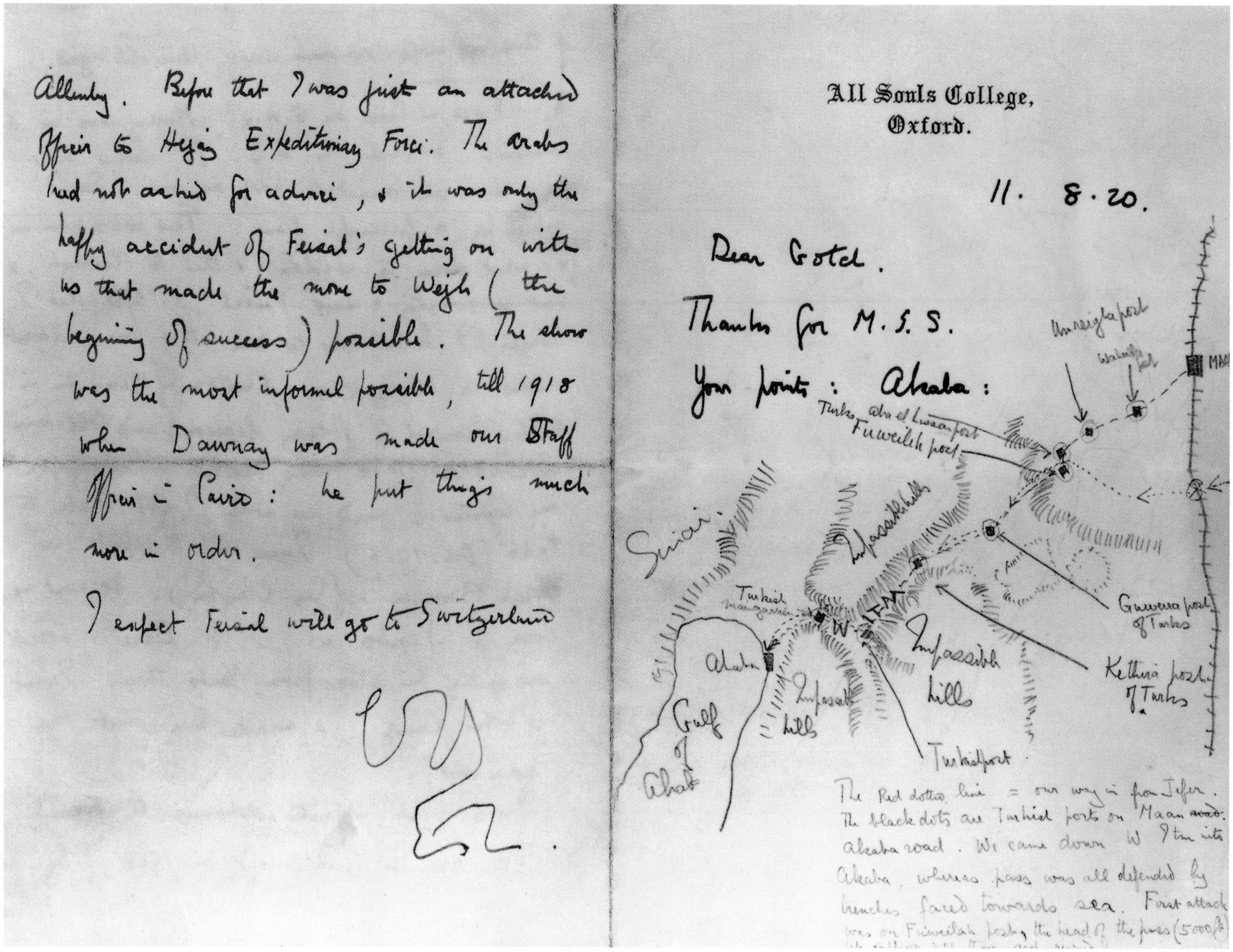

Allenby. Before that I was just an attached
Officer to Hejaz Expeditionary Force. The Arabs
had not asked for advice, & it was only the
happy accident of Feisal's getting on with
us that made the move to Wejh (the
beginning of success) possible. The show
was the most informal possible, till 1918
when Dawnay was made our Staff
Officer in Cairo : he put things much
more in order.

I expect Feisal will go to Switzerland

All Souls College,
Oxford.

11 . 8 . 20 .

Dear Gotch .
Thanks for M. S. S.
Your points : Akaba :

The Red dotted line = our way in from Jefer.
The black dots are Turkish posts on Maan road.
Akaba road . We came down W. Ithm into
Akaba, whereas pass was all defended by
trenches faced towards sea. First attack
was on Fuweilah post, the head of the pass (5000ft)

A fascinating hark-back to Akaba from 1920, when Lawrence was at All Souls College, Oxford, struggling to write his account of the desert campaign. A former map officer at Cairo, Leonard Gotch, wrote to him stating that he wanted to lecture about Lawrence's exploits. Lawrence obliged by sending him a four-page letter, including maps showing, left, a close-up of the situation at Akaba, July 1916, and, right, a map showing both the position of Akaba in relation to Wejh, and, more significantly, the actual route taken by Lawrence and his detachment in order to attack Akaba from the rear.

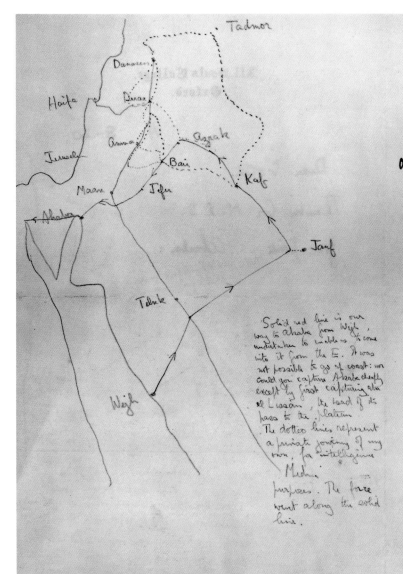

Solid red line is our way to Akaba from Wejh, undertaken to enable us to come into it from the E. It was not possible to go up coast: nor could you capture Akaba cheaply except by first capturing Abu el Lissan, the head of its pass to the plateau. The dotted lines represent a private journey of my own, for intelligence purposes. The force went along the solid line.

If these two maps don't make clear, please write again.

II. I was in Cairo on G.H.Q. Murray was in Ismailia. Holdich, his G.S.O. "I" didn't like my manners and meant to hoof me out. So I asked for a fortnight's leave. This was given me, [Oct. 1916] & I went down to Jidda, & then to Rabegh, & went up country & saw Feisal. After that I thought I knew how to run that war, & went across to Wingate in Khartoum (he was then in military control of Hejaz liaison) and told him all about it. He then asked Murray for my services: and so when I got back to Cairo (Oct. 1916) I was told to report to Arab Bureau: (Gen. Clayton). He sent me down to Yenbo as O i/c Base: Feisal was getting his stores from Yenbo then. I went up to his camp, & made him trust me somehow.

I was first appointed adviser to Feisal (for irregular operations) in 1918, by

Note that Lawrence's reply, while being remarkably detailed in relation to the attack on Akaba, is curiously vague, indeed actively misleading, in relation to his wartime role. His statement 'I was first appointed adviser to Feisal (for irregular operations) in 1918, by Allenby' is clearly a diminution of his status and influence, presumably reflecting his depressive mood at the time of writing. The maps, however, tell a different, and more accurate, story.

Lawrence and the Desert

One of a mass of photographs taken by Lawrence showing his fascination with the landscape of the desert.

'Bedouin ways were hard even for those brought up to them, and for strangers terrible: a death in life. When the march or labour ended I had no energy to record sensation, nor while it lasted any leisure to see the spiritual loveliness which sometimes came upon us by the way…

The abstraction of the desert landscape cleansed me, and rendered my mind vacant with its superfluous greatness; a greatness achieved not by the addition of thought to its emptiness, but by its subtraction. In the weakness of earth's life was mirrored the strength of heaven, so vast, so beautiful, so strong.'

SEVEN PILLARS OF WISDOM

'At first it had been grey shingle, packed like gravel. Then the sand increased and the stones grew rarer, till we could distinguish the colours of the separate flakes, porphyry, green schist, basalt. At last it was nearly pure white sand, under which lay a harder stratum. Such going was like a pile carpet for our camels' running. The particles of sand were clean and polished, and caught the blaze of sun like little diamonds in a reflection so fierce, that after a while I could not endure it. I frowned hard, and pulled the head-cloth forward in a peak over my eyes, and beneath them, too, like a beaver, trying to shut out the heat which rose in glassy waves off the ground, and beat up against my face.'

SEVEN PILLARS OF WISDOM

Approach to Wadi Rumm

Another of Lawrence's desert photographs, but one with a specific, important subject. The hills in the distance are the outcrop of one of his most favoured places in all Arabia, Wadi Rumm, effectively a waterless above-ground Grand Canyon a hundred miles long. Even 'the unsentimental Howeitat' thought of it as 'lovely', he claimed, while for his part he saw it as 'vast and echoing and God-like'. He later stated that he would sometimes 'turn aside to clear my senses by a night in Rumm'.

'Greater than imagination...'

Lawrence was moved and impressed by the often strange grandeur of the desert, as shown by his photograph, left, of Jebel el Sukhur, but nowhere more so than when visiting Wadi Rumm, pictured opposite.

'The crags were capped in nests of domes, less hotly red than the body of the hill; rather grey and shallow. They gave the finishing semblance of Byzantine architecture to this irresistible place: this processional way greater than imagination. The Arab armies would have been lost in the length and breadth of it, and within the walls a squadron of aeroplanes could have wheeled in formation. Our little caravan grew self-conscious and fell dead quiet, afraid and ashamed to flaunt its smallness in the presence of the stupendous hills.'

SEVEN PILLARS OF WISDOM

The Desert Campaign: an artist's interpretation

'It's a trifle… but the technique of dress, shapes of camels, seats of riders etc. are as right as if you had worked them up on the spot. I'm afraid that means that you have exhausted yourself in continual study of those photographs. However I'm enormously grateful.'

Lawrence to William Roberts,
11 December 1922

Camel March by William Roberts, specially painted for the subscribers' edition of *Seven Pillars of Wisdom*. Lawrence lent him photographs to help him with the details.

The narrow-gauge 'pilgrim' railway linking Damascus to Medina – railhead for the holy city of Mecca – which became a regular target for attack by Arab forces in 1917–18. The photograph shows a Turkish supply train at Kissir, south of Amman, 234 kilometres (145 miles) from Damascus. The railway itself was some 1380 kilometres (800 miles approximately) in length.

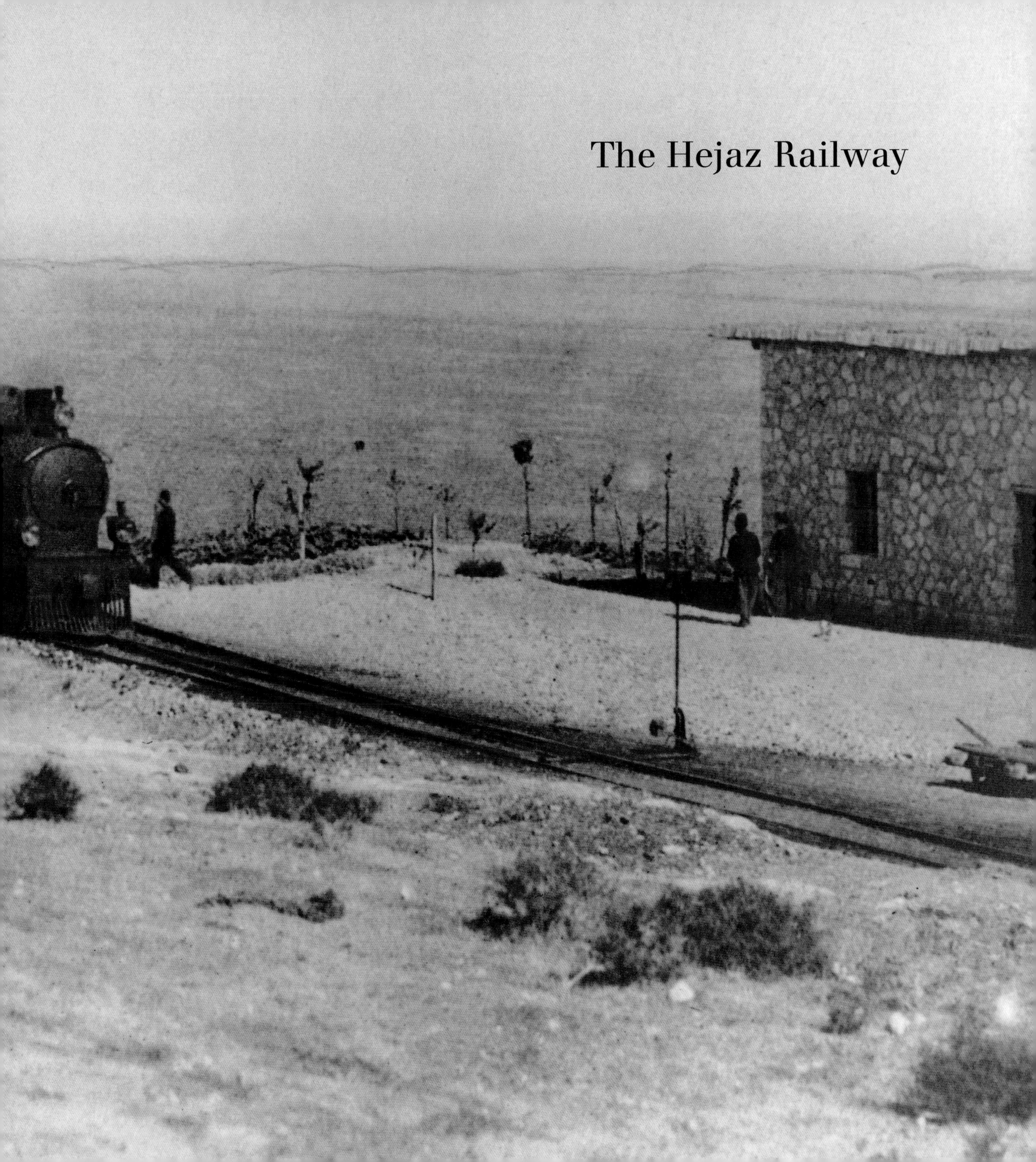
The Hejaz Railway

The Railway War

Opposite: The railway at Abu Taka. Significantly Lawrence, at least in the first stage of the campaign, attacked tracks rather than trains, to avoid unnecessary risks to his companions.

Below: A wrecked train from the Arab campaign, photographed in 1968.

'Governments saw men only in mass; but our men, being irregulars, were not formations, but individuals. An individual death, like a pebble dropped in water, might make but a brief hole; yet rings of sorrow widened out therefrom. We could not afford casualties.

In a railway-cutting it would usually be an empty stretch of rail; and the more empty, the greater the tactical success. We might turn our average into a rule... and develop a habit of never engaging the enemy.... Our cue was to destroy, not the Turk's army, but his minerals. The death of a Turkish bridge or rail, machine or gun or charge of high explosive, was more profitable to us than the death of a Turk.'

SEVEN PILLARS OF WISDOM

Contemporary evidence of the Arabs' efforts

Left: A ruined station.
Below: Turkish soldiers mending broken track, both photographs probably taken by Lawrence.

Lawrence had two attitudes to his railway raids, especially when enemy deaths became unavoidable. Thus to an army friend he wrote: 'I hope this sounds the fun it is… It's the most amateurish, Buffalo Billy sort of performance, and the only people who do it well are the Bedouin.' Yet on the previous day he had written to an Oxford colleague: 'I'm not going to last out this game much longer: nerves going and temper wearing thin, and one wants an unlimited account of both…. This killing and killing of Turks is horrible….'

Moving north

Left: Lawrence, standing right, photographed with two other officers during a raid into Turkish-held territory, 1917.

The rifle held by the officer, left of frame, is a Lee Enfield mark 3, similar to – indeed possibly the same as – the one pictured here: Lawrence's own rifle, inscribed on the butt 'T.E.L. 4.12.16', given to him by Feisal, to whom it had been donated before the Arab Revolt by the Turkish leader Enver Pasha, having been originally acquired at Gallipoli during the failed British campaign in 1915. In a letter dated December 1917, Lawrence stated that the Arab inscription read: 'Part of our booty in the battles for the Dardanelles.' Lawrence subsequently gave the rifle to King George V who in turn presented it to the Imperial War Museum.

The Castle at Azrak

'We are in an old fort with stone roofs and floors, and stone doors of the sort they used in Bashan. It is a bit out of repair, but is improving in that respect every day… I am staying here a few days; resting my camels, and then will have another fling. Last "fling" was two railway engines. One burst into fragments, and the other fell on the first. Quite a successful moment! If you see a note in print saying that "A detachment of the N[orthern] Army of Sherif Feisul etc." Then that's me….'

From a letter to his family, 14 November 1917

Left: The Castle at Azrak, in the desert east of Amman, where Lawrence was based for much of November 1917.

Below: The room in the castle at Azrak reputedly occupied by Lawrence. Both photographs taken by him.

'In these slow nights we were secure against the world… In the evening, when we had shut-to the gate, all guests would assemble…and coffee and stories would go round until the last meal, and after it, till sleep came. On stormy nights we brought in brushwood and dung and lit a great fire in the middle of the floor. About it would be drawn the carpets and the saddle-sheepskins, and in its light we would tell over our own battles, or hear the visitors' tradition. The leaping flames chased our smoke-ruffled shadows strangely about the rough stone wall behind us, distorting them over the hollows and projections of its broken face… Past and future flowed over us like an uneddying river. We dreamed ourselves into the spirit of the place; sieges and feasting, raids, murders, love-singing in the night.'

SEVEN PILLARS OF WISDOM

Jerusalem…
'the greatest moment'

Opposite: General Allenby's triumphal entry into Jersualem after its seizure from the Turks. In deference to the sanctity of the city, he walked rather than rode.

Above: A group of Allied officers photographed before the formal entry. The short British officer in the background, third from left, in – unusually for him – army uniform, borrowed for the occasion, is T. E. Lawrence. Although not involved in the capture of the city, he hailed it as 'the greatest moment of the war'.

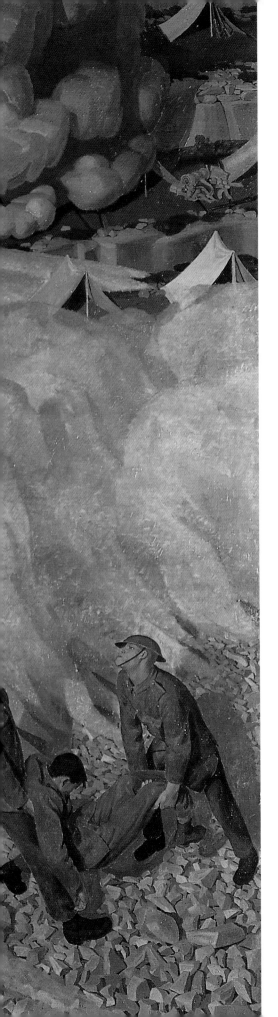

The Campaign in Palestine

Irish Troops in the Judean Hills Surprised by a Turkish Bombardment, a painting by Henry Lamb, dating from 1919, and chosen by Lawrence as an illustration for *Seven Pillars of Wisdom*. As the product of a specific commission by the Ministry of Information to paint a 'Palestine subject', its virtue is that it acts as a reminder that the main burden of the Middle Eastern campaign was born by the regular soldiers of the Middle East Expeditionary Force in Palestine, rather than the irregulars fighting in the desert with whom Lawrence served. His inclusion of it in his book can be seen as an acknowledgment of that fact, even if, as is evident from the quotation below, he harboured intellectual doubts as to the necessity of all-out military attack.

'By careful persistence, kept strictly within our strength and following the spirit of our theories, we were able eventually to reduce the Turks to helplessness, and complete victory seemed to be almost within our sight when General Allenby by his immense stroke in Palestine threw the enemy's main forces into hopeless confusion and put an immediate end to the Turkish war. We were very happy to have done with all our pains, but sometimes since I have felt a private regret that his too-greatness deprived me of the opportunity of following to the end the dictum of Saxe that a war might be won without fighting battles.'

From 'The Evolution of a Revolt',
published in the ARMY QUARTERLY, *October 1920*

Tafileh – spoils of battle

Austrian guns captured at Tafileh, south of the Dead Sea, January 1918, in the nearest Lawrence ever got to a conventional battle. A headlong Turkish attack produced 400 Turkish dead and 250 prisoners, the Arab casualties being 25 dead and 40 wounded. Praised in the Official History of the war as 'a brilliant feat of arms', it did not satisfy Lawrence who felt it and its crop of casualties could have been avoided. 'There was no glory left,' he wrote, 'but the terror of the broken flesh, which had been our own men, carried past us to their homes.' His report on the action delighted Headquarters, which 'to crown the jest, offered me a decoration on the strength of it'. He commented, wryly: 'We should have more bright breasts in the Army if each man was able without witnesses, to write out his own despatch.'

'Fellows were very proud of being in my bodyguard, which developed a professionalism almost flamboyant. They dressed like a bed of tulips, in every colour but white; for that was my constant wear and they did not wish to seem to presume.... They would travel day or night at my whim, and made it a point of honour never to mention fatigue.... In my service nearly sixty of them died.'

SEVEN PILLARS OF WISDOM

Lawrence and his bodyguard

Lawrence with some of the 'picked riders' who served with him for much of 1918. Photographed in Akaba, with Lawrence (not on this occasion wearing white) standing centre.

Men who rode with Lawrence

Pastel portraits by
Eric Kennington, 1921
Left: Mahmas ibn Dakhil:
'A tight-lipped youth with
pointed chin and pointed
forehead, whose beady
eyes dropped at the
inner corners with an
indescribable air of
impatience. He was not
properly of my guard, but
a camel-driver… and a
constantly-hurt pride made
him sudden and fatal in
companionship. If worsted
in argument, or laughed
at, he would lean forward
with his always handy
little dagger and rip up
his friend.' (*Seven Pillars
of Wisdom*)

Opposite: Muttar il
Hamoud Min Bini Hassan.
'Muttar, a parasite fellow of
the Beni Hassan, attached
himself to us. His fat
peasant's buttocks filled
his camel-saddle, and took
nearly as large a share
in the lewd or lurid jokes
which, on march, helped
pass my guards' leisure…
His unblushing greed made
us sure of him, till his
expectations failed.' (*Seven
Pillars of Wisdom*)

'Fighting de luxe'

Below: The second phase of the desert campaign, after Akaba, saw the deployment of armoured cars, which added pace and dash to the desert campaign. Lawrence dubbed this 'fighting de luxe'. The car featured is a Rolls Royce. Lawrence travelled many hundreds of miles in his own Rolls Royce tender, which he dubbed 'Blue Mist'. Despite prolonged usage over rough terrain, over eighteen months it had only one structural breakdown.

'Great was Rolls, and great was Royce! They were worth hundreds of men to us in these deserts.'

SEVEN PILLARS OF WISDOM

Opposite: A strange sight in Wadi Itm in March 1918: a Talbot motor car, with, among the passengers, Auda standing left, Feisal seated right. The identity of the driver is uncertain.

Warfare in the air

Left and below left:
Biplanes of the Royal Flying Corps (merged with the Royal Naval Air Service to become the Royal Air Force on 1 April 1918), which played a significant role in the later stages of the desert campaign. Their function comprised reconnaissance, communication, bombing and the provision of air cover. They excited much curiosity: the photograph below left shows an Arab inspecting the modified Lewis gun of a Bristol F.2B.

Opposite: This photograph of a crashed BE12 biplane, taken by Lawrence, commemorates air power at its best and its most vulnerable. Its pilot, a Lieutenant Junor, had provided air cover for an attack on the Yarmuk section of the railway link to Palestine in September 1918, to find himself under attack on three sides by enemy aircraft. He was forced to make a crash landing. He had just got out from his cockpit when a Turkish aircraft dropped a bomb on it.

Air warfare in art

Opposite: *The Sea of Galilee: Aeroplanes Attacking Turkish Boats*, by Sydney Carline, 1919.

Right: *The Destruction of the Turkish Transport in the Gorge of Wadi Fara, Palestine*, by Sydney Carline, 1920.

Lawrence later described this event as a 'climax of air attack' and a 'holocaust of the miserable Turks', adding: 'When our cavalry entered the silent valley next day they could count ninety guns, fifty lorries, nearly a thousand carts abandoned with all their belongings. The R.A.F. lost four killed. The Turks lost a corps.'

REVOLT IN THE DESERT

Opposite: Photography from the air: a striking reconnaissance photograph showing the railway station of Mudawwara, bottom right, target for a major raid in July 1918.

Right: *Damascus and the Lebanon Mountains from 10,000 feet,* by Richard Carline, Damascus at the bottom of the frame.

Aerial view of the target of the Arab Campaign: *Damascus*, by Richard Carline. Effectively a striking 'cut to close-up', in relation to the painting on page 119.

The end of the line

The Terminus of the Hejaz
Railway at Damascus,
fired by the Turks on
30 September 1918 before
abandoning the city.

The final days: October 1918

Opposite: Lawrence in 'Blue Mist' in Damascus, which he reached on 1 October. His attitude and general appearance suggest a man on the edge of exhaustion.

Above: Arrival in Damascus of the Commander-in-Chief, General Allenby, seated next to the driver, 3 October. Allenby brought the news that Feisal was not to be allowed the apotheosis he and Lawrence had hoped for, and that Syria would effectively become a fiefdom of the French.

Damascus captured

Arab troops in the city,
1 October 1918

'*Sherif Nasir with Major Stirling and myself moved into Damascus at 9 a.m. on October 1st amid scenes of extraordinary enthusiasm on the part of the local people. The streets were nearly impassable with the crowds, who yelled themselves hoarse, danced, cut themselves with swords and daggers and fired volleys in the air. Nasir, Nuri Shalaan, Auda Abu Tayi and myself were cheered by name, covered with flowers, kissed indefinitely, and splashed with attar of roses.*'

*Lawrence to General Staff, G.H.Q.,
from Damascus, 1 October 1918*

Damascus liberated

The main square, 2 October 1918: British supply lorries, plus an Arab patrol; people of the city looking on.

Damascus in transition

Arab troops, camel-mounted, passing a group of Turkish prisoners.

'*The streets were full of the debris of the broken army.... Typhus, dysentery and pellagra were rife.... Nuri prepared scavenger gangs to make a first clearing of the pestilent roads and open places.*'

SEVEN PILLARS OF WISDOM

Feisal at Damascus

Opposite: Damascus:
Feisal's headquarters.
His flag flies from the
balcony; an impromptu
gallows awaits traitors.

Above: Feisal leaving
the Hotel Victoria, after
his unsatisfactory meeting
with Allenby, 3 October.
With Lawrence as aide
and adviser, he would
take the Arab cause to
the councils of Europe.

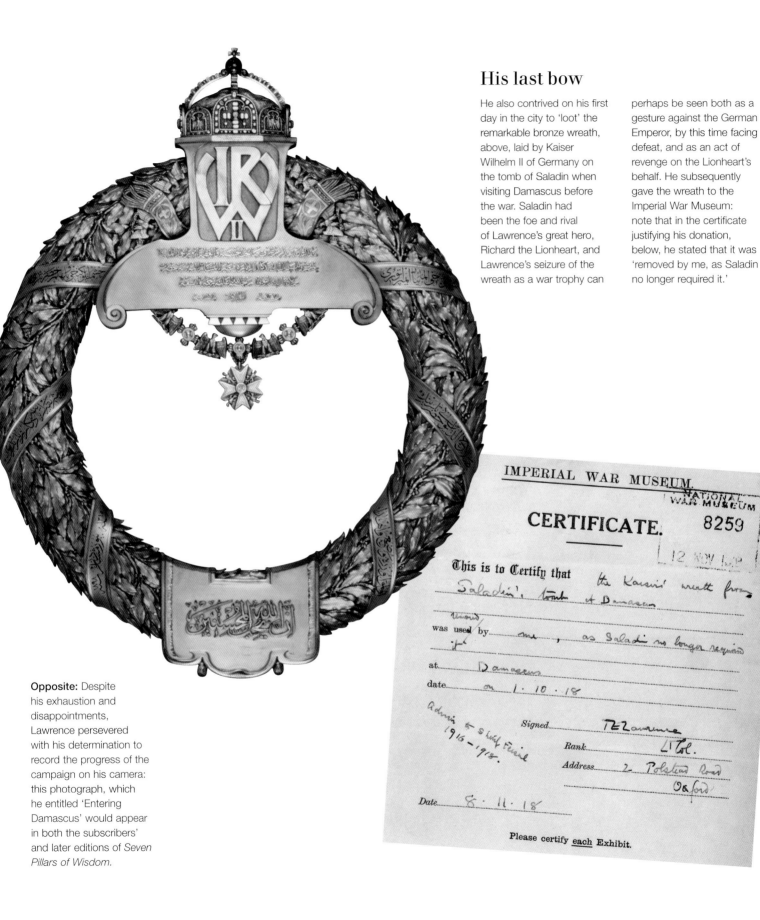

His last bow

He also contrived on his first day in the city to 'loot' the remarkable bronze wreath, above, laid by Kaiser Wilhelm II of Germany on the tomb of Saladin when visiting Damascus before the war. Saladin had been the foe and rival of Lawrence's great hero, Richard the Lionheart, and Lawrence's seizure of the wreath as a war trophy can perhaps be seen both as a gesture against the German Emperor, by this time facing defeat, and as an act of revenge on the Lionheart's behalf. He subsequently gave the wreath to the Imperial War Museum: note that in the certificate justifying his donation, below, he stated that it was 'removed by me, as Saladin no longer required it.'

Opposite: Despite his exhaustion and disappointments, Lawrence persevered with his determination to record the progress of the campaign on his camera: this photograph, which he entitled 'Entering Damascus' would appear in both the subscribers' and later editions of *Seven Pillars of Wisdom*.

IMPERIAL WAR MUSEUM.

NATIONAL WAR MUSEUM

CERTIFICATE.   8259

12 NOV 19

This is to Certify that   the Kaiser's wreath from Saladin's tomb at Damascus

was used by   me, as Saladin no longer required it

at   Damascus

date   on 1·10·18

Admin of S Wilf Feisul 1916–1918

Signed   TELawrence

Rank   LtCol.

Address   2 Polstead Road Oxford

Date   8·11·18

Please certify *each* Exhibit.

Countdown to departure

Left: Lawrence on the balcony of a Damascus hotel, 2 October 1918, two days before he left to continue his fight for the Arabs by other means.

Opposite: Lawrence at Damascus, 3 October 1918; portrait by James McBey. Many years later McBey, living at that time in Tangier, Morocco, wrote eloquently of the occasion, in a letter to Lowell Thomas, quoted below.

'During the sitting one after another of those bearded chieftains gently opened the door of the room where I was working, tiptoed across to Lawrence and kissed his right hand as it lay on the arm of the chair. Tears were on the cheeks of some of them. These tears may have been… part of a farewell ritual (I have seen the technique used here on occasions). Nevertheless it happened, and I saw it. Lawrence showed no reaction, but kept his pose for me admirably.'

James McBey to Lowell Thomas, 9 March 1954

'We were an odd little set, and we have, I expect, changed History in the Near East. I wonder how the Powers will let the Arabs get on.'

Lawrence to a fellow officer, October 1918

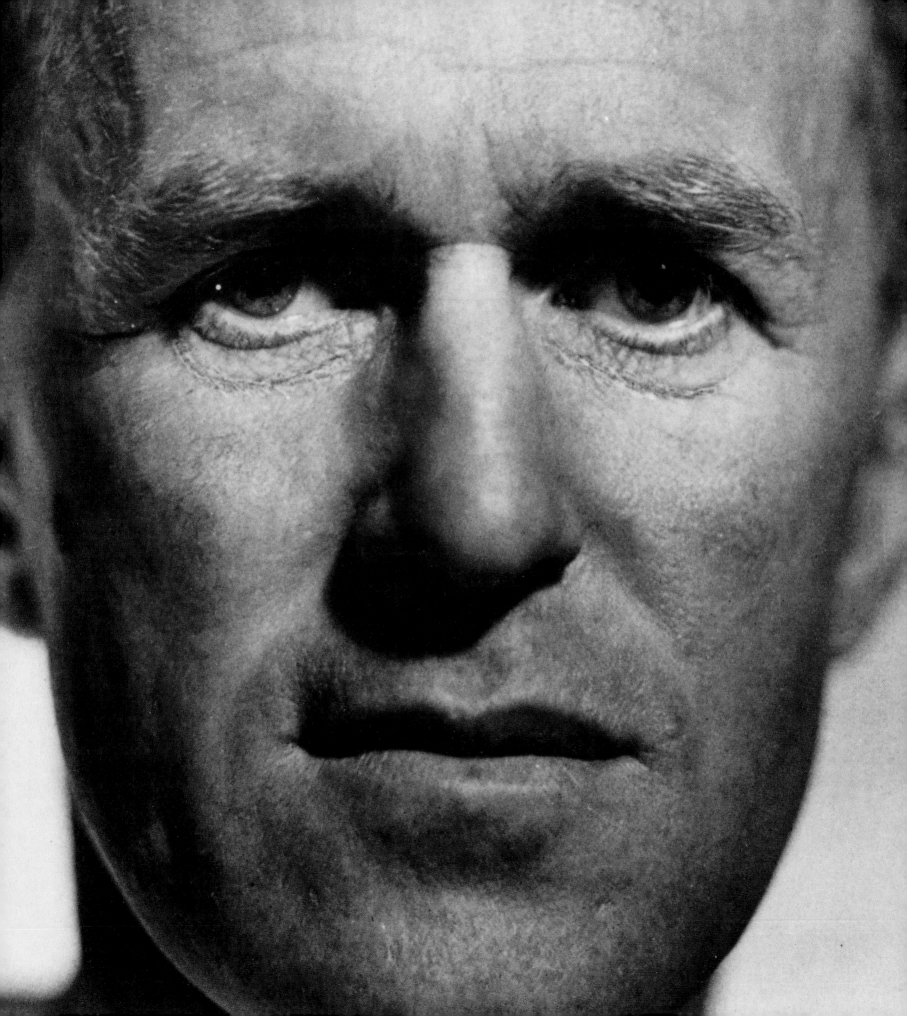

THE WILDERNESS YEARS

PART 3

A studio portrait by the well-known photographer, Howard Coster, one of a series taken in London in 1931.

The 'amusing job' Lawrence had anticipated two years earlier had proved to be a far more troubled and complex one than he anticipated. During the war, however, there was an overriding, unifying task, a target with a definite, geographical location. Now, back in London, he was facing an altogether more complex situation and facing it alone; hurrying around the political venues of the Empire's capital, battling across the table rather than in the field, the enemies to be outwitted being civilian not military ones and, officially, on his own side. On 21 October he appeared before the War Cabinet's Eastern Committee, whose chairman was the illustrious former Viceroy of India, Lord Curzon, now serving as a senior minister under the British Premier David Lloyd George. He soon learned that his name was already known in London's ruling circles when Curzon opened by stating that 'he and every member of His Majesty's Government had for some time watched with interest and admiration the great work which Colonel Lawrence had been doing in Arabia, and felt proud that [he] had done so much to promote the successful progress of the British and the Arab arms.' When invited to give his own views, Lawrence did so without equivocation. He wanted to see the leaders of the Arab Revolt – whom

Lawrence and Feisal photographed on board the battleship HMS *Orion*, during a courtesy visit to Scotland in December 1918. The visit gave Feisal the opportunity to thank the Royal Navy for its support during the Arabian campaign.

he named as Feisal, Abdullah, and their younger brother, Zeid, who had played a distinct if somewhat wayward part in the campaign in 1918 – given their own area of rule in the Middle East. The great men listened and were amazed. His plans as expounded at this and a later meeting some days later were minuted as representing 'the extreme Arab view', the kind of thing Feisal 'would have said had he been at our table that afternoon.' The elegant coolness of the comment indicated the minimal prospects of the concept being realized.

Apart from other factors, the timing of his efforts to trumpet the Arab cause could not have been less propitious. As October gave way to November the nation's attention was fixed on the imminent prospect of victory in Europe. In particular, the hope of an end to the war of the Western Front, which had produced so many dramas and so many deaths, pushed all other subjects to the sidelines. Nevertheless Lawrence kept up his one-man campaign. A document officially date-stamped by the War Office on 5 November shows him trying again, with a three-page printed submission entitled 'Reconstruction of Arabia', signed, as it happened – someone must have misread his doubtless hurried handwriting – 'T. E. LAURENCE, Lieut. Colonel'. In it he hailed the courage of the Meccan ruling family for their rallying to the Allied cause, pointing out 'the moral ordeal it has been for the oldest, most holy, and most powerful family of the Arabs (a people who lay more stress on faith and pedigree than others), to cast off the friends and allegiances of a lifetime and to incur, on behalf of their national freedom, the unmeasured abuse of India, Turkey, Afghanistan and Egypt.' He urged that wartime plans for division of the area between Britain and France should be abandoned, since, he claimed, they would now be 'laughed out of court' on account of their 'geographical absurdities'. If they were not so discarded, he wrote in a final pregnant sentence, 'I hope that we will at least recognize our official inclusion of the Arabs among the belligerents, and make them a party to any decisions affecting the Arab area conquered by themselves.'

Thus was established the doctrine for which he was to give so much effort and energy for the next three years. There were some successes. It was formally agreed that Feisal should be invited as a delegate to the forthcoming peace conference, due to assemble in Paris in January 1919. It was also agreed that Lawrence should go with him

Feisal, centre, with Lawrence behind him to his left, photographed during the Paris Peace Conference, 22 January 1919. Also present, left to right: Feisal's personal secretary; Nuri Said (later Prime Minister of Iraq); Capitaine Pisani, commander of the French gunnery detachment with Feisal's army; Captain Hassan Kadri; at the back, Feisal's slave.

as his special aide. Here, at last, the Arab voice was heard, as the two men, punching well above their weight, became a conference phenomenon, with an impressive Feisal appearing in his best Oriental finery and Lawrence ever beside him in his colonel's uniform topped by an Arab head-dress. 'I have seen 10 American newspaper men, and given them all interviews,' Lawrence wrote home; 'also President Wilson, and the other people who have influence.' They made a considerable impact when on 6 February they had their chance to plead their cause before the conference's eminent 'Council of Ten', with Lawrence, as Feisal's interpreter, responding to great effect when asked to repeat Feisal's message in French for those delegates with inadequate English. As he concluded, the members of the Council broke into spontaneous applause. An observer wrote: 'They had started the session as conscious arbiters of the state of mankind; they were ending it as a captive audience of a minor suppliant's interpreter.'

It was a fine moment, but it would cut little ice in the councils of the major powers. To Lawrence, speaking not just on his own behalf but of all those who had borne the brunt of over four years war only to see the soldiers handing over the stage to the statesmen, this was symptomatic of the whole way in which the political decisions of the post-war world would be made. Essentially, he spoke not just for his war, but all wars. The passage would appear in the opening pages of *Seven Pillars of Wisdom*:

*We lived many lives in those whirling campaigns, never sparing
ourselves: yet when we achieved and the new world dawned,
the old men came out again and took our victory to re-make
in the likeness of the former world they knew. Youth could win,
but had not learned to keep: and was pitiably weak against
age. We stammered that we had worked for a new heaven and
a new earth, and they thanked us kindly and made their peace.*

Meanwhile he had a home life to return to. But the house in Polstead Road had already lost two of its members killed in France and there would soon be another fatality. In April 1919 Lawrence's father suddenly fell victim to the current worldwide influenza pandemic. It was almost certainly at this juncture that a letter his father had written

THE LOWELL THOMAS TRAVELOGUES

WITH ALLENBY IN PALES.
and LAWRENCE IN ARAB
UNDER DIRECTION OF DALE CARNAGE
"ON NO STAGE AS BE N SENTER ANYTHIN MORE F SCINATING"

'A remarkable film lecture telling the strange story of Colonel Thomas Lawrence, the leader of the Arab Army. A large number of well-known personalities gathered on the opening night to hear Mr Lowell Thomas's film lecture on the Palestine campaign.'

from an account in THE SPHERE *of the opening lecture at the Royal Opera House, Covent Garden, 1919*

exposing the details of the family background was shown to him. Throughout the boys' childhood the family had seemed a happy one, but a retrospective shadow must surely have been cast by a passage towards the end of the letter which read: 'I can say no more, except that there never was a truer saying than "the ways of transgressors are hard". Take warning from the terrible anxieties and sad thoughts endured by both yr Mother and me for now over thirty years!'

There were other pressures. He had already started his account of his wartime experiences in Paris and now it became a paramount obsession. Oxford's All Souls College appointed him to a Fellowship to give him academic peace and security in order to accomplish this task, but, with a curious perversity that made him wary of becoming part of any establishment however benign, he found a more congenial place in which to write in a garret room in Westminster, London, loaned to him by an architect friend, Sir Herbert Baker. The summer of 1919 brought a pressure of a different kind when Lowell Thomas, the American publicist he had met in Jerusalem and subsequently in the desert, astounded

Poster for the first 'Lowell Thomas Travelogues', New York, 1919; later exported to Britain and subsequently to become an international sensation. Although initially the focus was on Allenby with Lawrence in a lesser role, audience response soon gave Lawrence precedence. Thereafter the change of preposition, from 'Lawrence *in*' to 'Lawrence *of* Arabia', was virtually inevitable.

Above: Lawrence with Lowell Thomas, in Arabia 1918: originally a black and white photograph, tinted for use in Lowell Thomas's entertainment. Taken by Harry Chase, who combined the roles of Thomas's photographer and film cameraman.

London with, to quote a report of the time, 'a Remarkable Film Lecture Telling the Strange Story of Colonel Thomas Lawrence, the Leader of the Arab Army'. More show than lecture, Thomas's entertainment, which included music and dance as well as film, had originally meant to celebrate General Allenby, but soon focused on the more dashing figure of the junior man. Opening in Covent Garden it was later transferred to the Royal Albert Hall. In this way 'Lawrence of Arabia' was born, and though there was gratification in the fame this brought it also turned him into a quasi-film star, tying on to him a celebrity which he later compared to 'a tin can attached to a cat's tail.'

Right: Lowell Thomas, again by Harry Chase.

Below: A page of one of his scripts, in which he ranked Lawrence with some of the great figures of British imperial history, and included the kind of anecdote with which he kept his audiences entertained.

14.

The Turks and Germans offered rewards of ovr £50,000 on the head of this young archeologist

SLIDE 224   dead or alive! But the Arabs wouldn't have given him up for over £500,000 because they realised that their chance of throwing off the Turkish yoke depended to a grat extent upon the ability of this modest

SLIDE 225.   youth. Notice the difference between the way Lawrence is squatting and the way his companion is seated. He became so accustomed to living in the desert with the Arabs that he actually preferred to squat down as they do instead of sitting in a chair.

SLIDE 226.   And I believe that this young man who built up the Arabian army and liberated Holy Arabia will go down in history

SLIDE 227.   alongside of such picturesque figures as Francis Drake, Clive, "Chinese" Gordon and Kitchener of Khartoum.

SLIDE 228.   The Germans sent many airplanes down to Arabia in an attempt to frighten Lawrence's army. But instead of their having that effect they simply caused the Arabs to insist on Lawrence getting airplanes for them.

SLIDE 229.   One day the King of the Hedjaz sent Lawrence a message which read — "Oh, faithful one, thy country hast airplanes as the locusts. Please send us a dozen."

SLIDE 230.   This is one of the machines that he brought down from Egypt for them. One day the Arabs shot down a German plane with their rifles, and when it landed in the desert they ran out and clipped off its wings so that it wouldn't fly away!

A selection of
Lowell Thomas's
highly dramatic slides:

Above left: Camel train
in the desert, Lowell
Thomas, camel mounted,
in the foreground.

Above right: A sandstorm

Left: Sunset over the desert

Opposite: The man
whom Thomas hailed
as an 'Uncrowned King':
see overleaf.

$250,000 REWARD! DEAD OR ALIVE!
For the Capture of this Mystery Man of the East.

THE MOST AMAZING REVELATION OF A PERSONALITY
SINCE STANLEY FOUND LIVINGSTONE

(Reprinted from "Asia Magazine" — New York)

"Only once in a lifetime does a man — even a world traveler of broad adventure — meet with such experiences as Lowell Thomas encountered in Palestine and Arabia. For only once in a lifetime are the supernatural qualities of mankind brought out as they were in T. E. Lawrence, a mere youth of twenty-six, who became the uncrowned King of the Arabs as he led them against the Turks.

"The Story of Lawrence as revealed by Lowell Thomas is the most amazing revelation of a personality in the Great War. Here was a mere youngster, a reticent scholar of archaeology, with the love of liberty of his Irish ancestry, whose choice was to hide himself off alone in the deserts of Arabia exploring ruins. Suddenly he heard the call of war, entered the British army and disappeared into the desert again. Without a day of military training, even defying military rule, he was next heard of as the confidential adviser of the strong-willed King of the Hejaz, the organizer and leader of his Arab armies, followed implicitly by the Arabs as the bearer of a charmed life and of more than human wisdom.

"Only one person — an American who was associated with him in the Arabian desert — has been able to give us the full story of Lawrence's achievements. As related by Lowell Thomas it is a tale of wild adventure — colorful as the Arabian Nights, poetic as the Rubaiyat. It is not a story of war and slaughter but of a human being endowed with God-given powers. Indeed another Robert Clive has come — another Chinese Gordon — another Cortez."

> **MR. LLOYD GEORGE says:**
>
> "Everything that Mr. Lowell Thomas tells us about Colonel Lawrence is true. In my opinion, Lawrence is one of the most remarkable and romantic figures of modern times."

Left: A typical Lowell Thomas publicity spread.

Opposite: a heavily tinted version of a much used Lawrence image, with Lawrence's comment on his transfiguration, in a letter to his future American publisher.

Thomas was not a simplistic admirer of Lawrence, seeing ambiguity in his attitude to fame. He once described him, in a shrewd and memorable phrase, as 'backing into the limelight'.

'You know a Mr Lowell Thomas made me a kind of matinee idol: so I dropped my name as far as London is concerned and live peacefully in anonymity. Only my people in Oxford know of my address. It isn't that I hate being known – I'd love it – but I can't afford it: no-one gets so victimised by well-meaning people as a poor celebrity.'

Letter to F. N. Doubleday,
20 March 1920

Left: Delegates from the Cairo Conference on a visit to the Sphinx and the Pyramids, 20 March 1921. The group includes, left to right, Clementine Churchill, Winston Churchill, Gertrude Bell, and, wearing a trilby hat, Lawrence. Churchill was thrown by his camel, but nevertheless insisted on riding back to Cairo side by side with his young hero.

Right: The great and the good who settled the fate of the Middle East in 1921, with Churchill, seated centre, surrounded by his advisers, sometimes jokingly known as the 'forty thieves'; Lawrence stands behind him to his left.

He had thought himself through with the Middle East but when Winston Churchill became Colonial Secretary in 1921 he determined to remake the unsatisfactory settlement bequeathed by the powers in Paris and invited Lawrence to assist. He had no option but to comply. So Lawrence found himself back in places he had fought for during the war in the unlikely disguise of a trilby hat and a well-cut suit. Out of the subsequent negotiations Abdullah emerged as Emir of the territory that would eventually become the Kingdom of Jordan, while Feisal (who had earlier proclaimed himself King of Syria only to be deposed by the French) was compensated by the throne of Mesopotamia, now increasingly being known as Iraq. Lawrence came home confident enough to affirm that 'we were quit of our war-time Eastern adventure, with clean hands', but even after so much effort, there remained at least the hint of an undertow of doubt.

1 : RECRUITING OFFICE

GOD, this is awful. Hesitating for two hours up and down a filthy street, lips and hands and knees tremulously out of control, my heart pounding in fear of that little door through which I must go to join up. Try sitting a moment in the churchyard? That's caused it. The nearest lavatory, now. Oh yes, of course, under the church. What was Baker's story about the cornice?

A penny; which leaves me fifteen. Buck up, old seat-wiper: I can't tip you and I'm urgent. Won by a short head. My right shoe is burst along the welt and my trousers are growing fringes. One reason that taught me I wasn't a man of action was this routine melting of the bowels before a crisis. However, now we end it. I'm going straight up and in.

★

All smooth so far. They are gentle-spoken to us, almost sorry. Won't you walk into my parlour? Wait upstairs for medical exam? 'Righto!' This sodden pyramid of clothes upon the floor is sign of a dirtier man than me in front. My go next? Everything off? (Naked we come into the R.A.F.). Ross? 'Yes, that's me.'

Officers, two of them. . . .

'D'you smoke?'

Not much, Sir.

'Well, cut it out. See?'

Six months back, it was, my last cigarette. However, no use giving myself away.

'Nerves like a rabbit.' The scotch-voiced doctor's hard fingers go hammer, hammer, hammer over the loud box of my ribs. I must be pretty hollow.

13

Then, in August 1922, he astonished friends and critics alike by joining the Royal Air Force at the lowliest rank and under an assumed name. The struggles of a less than fit, over-age Aircraftman John Hume Ross to cope with the rigours of the RAF's training camp at Uxbridge gave him the subject for his second book, *The Mint*, so packed with the vernacular of the parade ground and the barrack room that it was not printed in an unexpurgated edition until the 1970s. Most vehement in expressing his outraged amazement at what he saw as Lawrence's absurd gesture was the playwright George Bernard Shaw, who had been asked by Lawrence to read an early version of *Seven Pillars*: 'Nelson slightly cracked after his whack on the head after the battle of the Nile, coming home and

Right: Lawrence as Aircraftman John Hume Ross of the Royal Air Force, 1922–23; oil painting by William Roberts.

Left: Bovington Camp, Dorset, where Lawrence served from March 1923 to August 1925.

Opposite: Lawrence wearing a bombardier's tunic that must have been borrowed. By an unknown photographer, *c.* 1924.

'And why I enlisted? The security of it first: seven years existence guaranteed. I haven't any longer the mind to fight for sustenance. As you realise I've finished with the "Lawrence" episode. I don't like what rumour makes of him – not the sort of man I'd like to be! and the life of politics wearied me out, by worrying me over-much. I've not got a coarse-fibred enough nature for them; and have too many scruples and an uneasy conscience. It's not good to see two sides of questions, when you have (officially) to follow one.

Exit politics… There went most of my money value. Exit Lawrence: and there is most of the residue of my earning power gone. I haven't a trade to follow: and won't do the two or three things for which I'm "qualified": hence I'm reduced to soldiering. You see, I'm 35 nearly: and that's too old to make a fresh start in a skilled business.'

Lawrence to D. G. Hogarth, 13 June 1923

insisting on being placed at the tiller of a canal barge and on being treated as nobody in particular would have embarrassed the Navy far less.' Shaw thought the whole business a 'maddening masquerade', but to Lawrence it was a necessary act of self-humiliation, a 'brain sleep' for a man overwrought by too many years of strain and effort compounded by an inescapable sense of guilt and failure.

Before long the British press, for whom Lawrence was now natural prey, found him, not at Uxbridge but at his second posting, the RAF School of Photography at Farnborough. The subsequent Fleet Street furore had him out of the Air Force within days, but like an escaper on the run he resorted to a second alias, Thomas Edward Shaw (there was, he claimed, no connection to the playwright in his choice), reappearing in March 1923 as a recruit to the Army at the Tank Corps training centre at Bovington, Dorset.

This was as low a point as he ever reached; letters poured from him, especially to his All Souls College friend, Lionel Curtis, indicating a mind almost at the end of its tether. About this time he instituted the floggings he kept hidden throughout his life but which deeply shocked his surviving friends when they became known over thirty years later. Punishment for guilt real or assumed? Flagellation medieval-style? Sado-masochism? A delayed response to the agony, and strange ecstasy, of Deraa? The true answers can never be known. Two factors held him from total depression: his passion for motorcycling (his choice was the best model going, the famous, much coveted 'Brough Superior', of which he ran through no fewer than seven versions); and the discovery of the tiny Dorset cottage near the camp which became his bolt-hole and sanctum for the rest of his life: Clouds Hill. The cottage also provided a suitable venue for a major attempt to finish *Seven Pillars*, which he planned not as a work for general publication, but as a highly crafted, lavishly illustrated limited edition for special subscribers only.

But Army life was no substitute for the Air Force, for which he still craved; he even resorted to hints of suicide to persuade the authorities to let him re-enlist. Back in the uniform he loved he was posted to RAF Cranwell, a station so genial in comparison to Uxbridge that it would enable him to complete *The Mint* in a mood that was almost mellow. Hence that strange book's remarkably benign final sentence: 'Everywhere a relationship: no loneliness any more'.

'...I've been wondering about the other fellows in the hut. A main feeling they give me is of difference from the RAF men. There we were excited about our coming service. We talked and wondered of the future, almost exclusively. There was a constant recourse to imagination, and a constant rewarding of ourselves therefore. The fellows were decent, but so wrought up by hope that they were carried out of themselves, and I could not see them mattly. There was a sparkle round the squad.

Here every man has joined because he was down and out: and no one talks of the Army or of promotion, or of trades and accomplishments. We are all here unavoidably, in a last resort, and we assume this world's failure in one-another, so that pretence would not be merely laughed at, but as near an impossibility as anything human. We are social bed-rock, those unfit for life-by-competition: and each of us values the rest as cheap as he knows himself to be.'

Letter to Lionel Curtis, 27 March 1923

He needed money to pay off debts accrued while printing *Seven Pillars*, so the idea of publishing a shorter popular version of *Seven Pillars* was conceived, with the more eye-catching title of *Revolt in the Desert*. He agreed the book should be described as by T. E. Lawrence, though distancing himself by locking the name in inverted commas, even he accepting that no one would make head or tail of 'T. E. Shaw' on the title page. But because of the huge interest the book would inevitably generate he asked the RAF to let him disappear. In December 1926 he sailed for India. He would be there for two years.

This was an act of deliberate retreat, but it was also a remarkably fruitful period of exile. During it he changed his name by deed poll to Thomas Edward Shaw. It was also at this time that he aired the idea of somehow becoming a Chapman again; to the chief executive of Oxford's Bodleian Library, on the matter of accessioning the copy of the subscribers' edition of *Seven Pillars* the library would shortly receive, he forecast they might have serious difficulties in cataloguing it in the future 'for not even Lawrence is the correct and authentic name which I will eventually have to resume. I've published as Lawrence, as Shaw, as Ross: and will, probably, eventually publish as C. What a life!'

Meanwhile he wrote book reviews, under another, strictly literary alias, Colin Dale, usually reduced to C.D.: adapted from the name of the

Opposite: Lawrence outside his Army hut at Bovington.

Above: Extract from one of the many unhappy letters he wrote during his two years as a Tank Corps private.

Below: His first published book, an abridged version of *Seven Pillars* under a deliberately popular title.

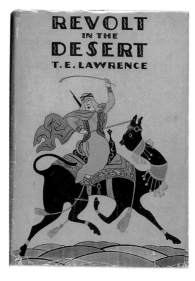

Above: The cottage at Clouds Hill. **Below:** The Greek inscription on the lintel, roughly meaning 'I don't care', was carved by Lawrence himself.

He once wrote of the cottage: 'It means that nothing in Clouds Hill is to be a care upon its habitant… Nothing to anchor me.'

'The cottage is alone in a dip in the moor – very quiet, very lonely, very bare, a mile from the camp. Furnished with a bed, a bicycle, three chairs, a hundred books, a gramophone and a table. Many windows, oak trees, rhododendron, laurels, heather. Dorsetshire to look at. I don't sleep here but come out 4.30 p.m. till 9.00 p.m. nearly every evening, and dream or write or read by the fire.'

Letter from Clouds Hill, 1924

Opposite: Part bolt-hole, part publishing house: it was here that Lawrence, with the help of numerous artists and experts in printing, compiled his elaborately designed subscribers' edition of *Seven Pillars of Wisdom.*

Above: A set of capital letters used in the book, designed by Edward Wadsworth.

Right: A sample page, beginning with Wadsworth's capital A, and including a drawing by William Roberts, one of many such sketches by various artists scattered through the book. The page also reflects Lawrence's insistence that every page should begin and end with a full sentence. He frequently adjusted his narrative to achieve this, yet when subsequently printed without such artifices the text showed few if any signs of deliberate manipulation.

Overleaf: The dedicatory poem printed at the beginning of every copy of *Seven Pillars of Wisdom.*

Feeling the Turks

AS I walked northward towards the fighting, Abdulla met me, on his way to Zeid with news. He had finished his ammunition, lost five men from shell-fire, and had one automatic gun destroyed. Two guns, he thought the Turks had. His idea was to get up Zeid with all his men and fight: so nothing remained for me to add to his message; and there was no subtlety in leaving alone my happy masters to cross and dot their own right decision.

He gave me leisure in which to study the coming battlefield. The tiny plain was about two miles across, bounded by low green ridges, and roughly triangular, with my reserve ridge as base. Through it ran the road to Kerak, dipping into the Hesa valley. The Turks were fighting their way up this road. Abdulla's charge had taken the western or left-hand ridge, which was now our firing-line.

Shells were falling in the plain as I walked across it, with harsh stalks of wormwood stabbing into my wounded feet. The enemy fuzing was too long, so that the shells grazed the ridge and burst away behind. One fell near me, and I learned its calibre from the hot cap. As I went they began to shorten range, and by the time I got to the ridge it was being freely sprinkled with shrapnel. Obviously the Turks had got observation somehow, and looking round I saw them climbing along the eastern side beyond the gap of the Kerak road. They would soon outflank us at our end of the western ridge.

460

DEDICATION
To S.A.

I loved you, so I drew these tides of men into my hands
and wrote my will across the stars
To earn you Freedom, the seven-pillared worthy house,
that your eyes might be shining for me
When we came.

Death seemed my servant on the road, til we were near
and saw you waiting:
When you smiled, and in sorrowful envy he outran me
and took you apart:
Into his quietness.

Love, the way-weary, groped to your body, our brief wage
ours for the moment
Before earth's soft hand explored your shape, and the blind
worms grew fat upon
Your substance.

Men prayed for me that I set our work, the inviolate house,
as a memory of you.
But for fit monument I shattered it, unfinished: and now
The little things creep out to patch themselves hovels
in the marred shadow
Of your gift.

Right: *The Poem to S.A.*, woodcut by Blair Hughes-Stanton, 1926. Hughes-Stanton contributed numerous sketches to the subscribers' edition, but this woodcut was not commissioned by Lawrence: it therefore represents the artist's unprompted response to this extraordinary poem. Lawrence nevertheless included it in a number of copies of the book. If anything it merely adds to the sense of mystery surrounding the poem, in the writing of which Lawrence was helped by his friend (and first biographer), the poet Robert Graves. For a brief discussion of the poem, and the possible identity of S.A, see Introduction.

'I consume the day (and myself) brooding and making phrases and reading, and thinking again, galloping mentally down twenty divergent roads at once… I sleep less than ever, for the quietness of night imposes thinking on me: I eat breakfast only, and refuse every possible distraction and employment and exercise. When my mood gets too hot and I find myself wandering beyond control I pull out my motor-bike and hurl it top-speed through these unfit roads for hour after hour. My nerves are jaded and gone near dead so that nothing less than hours of voluntary danger will pluck them into life, and the "life" they reach then is a melancholy joy at risking something worth exactly 2/9d a day.

It's odd, again, that craving for real risk: because in the gymnasium I funk jumping the horse, more than poison. That is physical, which is why it is: I'm ashamed of doing it and of not doing it, unwilling to do it: and most of all ashamed (afraid) of doing it well.'

Letter to Lionel Curtis, 14 May 1923

station, Colindale, nearest to the RAF aerodrome at Hendon, north London. With no new original book in prospect, he accepted a commission to translate the *Odyssey*. Equally significant, the two years produced an astonishingly rich crop of letters. Friendship had become a necessity to him at all levels and while far off in India could be maintained only by the pen. Those with whom he corresponded, often at considerable length, included John Buchan, E. M. Forster and Robert Graves; George Bernard Shaw and, especially, Shaw's wife Charlotte, by now and for the rest of his life Lawrence's closest confidante; Eric Kennington; his RAF boss, Sir Hugh Trenchard. Typically he also wrote long breezy letters to a former Cranwell comrade, Sergeant Pugh, ever concerned to 'ask kindly after Mrs Pugh, and Miss Pugh, and Tug and Dusty (though Dusty will now have left you).' If ever there was a man whose correspondence had no hierarchy it was T. E. Lawrence.

Lawrence on one
of his Brough Superior
motorcycles.

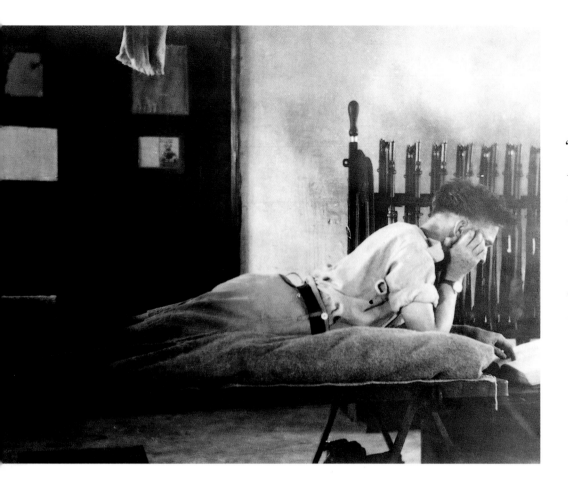

Left: Photograph of T. E. Lawrence in barracks at Miranshah Fort, *c.* 1928, sent to Charlotte Shaw. He wrote the message below on the back of the photograph.

'This is now my kingdom: my bed. A constitutional kingdom: for I may not change it nor arrange it except after a seated pattern. The book is Ulysses… Joyce's one. I heard the laughing little man preparing to snap me and changed from the left elbow to the right. The portrait is unrecognisable, I think but rather fun. The park paling effect behind my head is a rack of rifles. Under my book is a box of clothes. Over the top of the bed the edge of a mosquito net. Under the bed are boots! I hope you laugh.'

To minimize any chance of provoking publicity, he lived discreetly within the camp to which he was posted in Karachi (then part of India), confining himself voluntarily to barracks. In 1928 he was posted to Miranshah, far off on the Afghan border: 'almost the quietest place I have struck, in Stations,' he told Sergeant Pugh, adding: 'The place is so remote that not many people have heard of it.' Out of sight and almost out of mind, *Revolt in the Desert* became, inevitably, a best-seller.

And then a rebellion broke out in Afghanistan, and the discovery that the famous Lawrence of Arabia was lurking near its southern frontier under an assumed name was too good a story for any editor to resist, even though his most sinister activity at the time was the internationally unthreatening one of translating Homer. The inevitable lurid headlines suggesting that 'the arch spy of the world' (such indeed was his tabloid reputation) was up to his knavish tricks again presented the RAF with a problem they felt could only be resolved by

Opposite: Lawrence harked back rarely in his letters to his wartime years in Arabia, but this letter, written from India to Lieutenant Colonel F. G. Peake, who had served with him in the desert war and was now commander of the Arab Legion in Transjordan, is a distinct exception. Note its nostalgic reference to 'that delectable land' and his admission that he was 'often hungry for a sight of its hills. Rum, too. If only….'

Right: Lawrence in India at RAF Karachi, 1927: captioned by Robert Graves as 'Aircraftman Shaw in "Scruff Order"' in his biography, *Lawrence and the Arabs* (the forerunner to countless others), published in 1927.

Left: Lawrence on the airfield at RAF Miranshah: one of a series of photographs by Flight Lieutenant Smetham, commanding officer of a flight stationed there while Lawrence was in residence. It can be precisely dated to 10 December 1928.

Above: Presumed to show Lawrence on the SS *Rajputana*, on his way home from India, wearing a civilian suit lent him so as not to attract the attentions of the press.

whisking their extraordinary ordinary aircraftman away. They offered him Aden, Somaliland or home; he opted for home. The press was waiting for him en masse when the liner transporting him, the SS *Rajputana*, reached Plymouth Sound and he had to be spirited off the ship in a naval pinnace and hurried off into hiding.

Jaded and destabilized by all this, he was nevertheless about to enter one of his happiest times. The RAF officer who had managed his escape at Plymouth was Wing Commander Sydney Smith, whom he had met first during his Colonial Office activities, and who was commanding officer of the nearby seaplane base, RAF Cattewater. Posted there, Lawrence at once took to the place, whose name he and Smith soon had changed to the less risible, more salubrious one of RAF Mount Batten. Smith ran his station on a light rein, with his elegant and attractive wife, Clare, his daughter Maureen (alias 'Squeak') and

Above: Lawrence being taken off the *Rajputana* at Plymouth, early February 1929. So many boats hired by pressmen swarmed to meet the liner that it was decided to evacuate him by a rope-ladder on the seaward side. But the ladder caught on the hatch causing a delay and by the time he boarded the naval launch sent to collect him he had become an easy target for both still and newsreel cameras.

Left: In his last years in the RAF Lawrence prided himself on his practical work on such projects as the development of sophisticated RAF speedboats for air-sea rescue purposes. Many lives would be saved as a result of his and his colleagues' enterprise in the war he would not live to see.

their two dogs as much part of the community as the men. In effect it was less a service institution than a kind of extended family in which Lawrence soon became a virtual favourite uncle. Sydney Smith admired him and treated him as an equal. Clare fell in love with him, an affection fostered among other things by a shared interest in music – or more specifically in classical gramophone records, anathema to her musically illiterate husband. Before long the new arrival would find himself going out on regular boat excursions with Clare, activities which despite any suspicions to the contrary almost certainly culminated in nothing more newsworthy than a series of platonic picnics. There was an innocence in all this: Lawrence had never had many women friends and he was slow to realize the nature of Clare's affection, but there would also have been a bar of a different kind in that he was an 'other rank' in the service and the notion of an affair with his commanding officer's wife was one that would not have occurred to him. He would later confide to Lady Astor, another friend of his later years: 'Mrs Smith…wants from me something which I want to keep, and she ought to understand it,' adding 'There are Untouchables, thank Heaven, despite the Ghandi's of this world. Or is it Gandhi?…' Clare Sydney Smith later wrote a loving elegy to the time they shared together under the title of *The Golden Reign.* It says much both for Lawrence's innocence and his eloquence that the phrase was his coinage not hers.

Above: Lawrence with Wing Commander Sydney Smith, who became both his commanding officer and a close friend during Lawrence's final years in uniform.

'After having dabbled in revolt and politics it is rather nice to have been mechanically useful.'

Lawrence to Lord Lloyd,
fellow officer during the Arab Revolt,
26 September 1934

Right: While distancing himself from his earlier identity as 'Colonel Lawrence', he could still be approached by journalists eager to question him about his wartime past and especially about his dealings with the Arabs. To one such, an admiring American, he replied, via the RAF's Public Relations Officer, C. P. Robertson, who had forwarded the American's request:

'As for the Arabs, do tell your sportsman that he is out of date. It was about ten or twelve years ago and I've forgotten all about it. You handle Arabs, I think, as you handle Englishmen, or Laplanders or Czechoslovaks: cautiously, at first, and kindly always.'

However, the new posting had far more to offer than its social side. From the first he was caught up in work that excited and challenged him. Smith involved him in preparation work for the 1929 Schneider Cup Race, and subsequently – following the shock of a seaplane disaster in the Sound for which the craft available for searching for survivors were quite inadequate – they became involved in a serious, sustained campaign to produce fast new air-sea rescue boats. Herbert Read, in an incisive review of the subscribers' edition of *Seven Pillars of Wisdom* in 1928 tellingly wrote of Lawrence that he was 'a man with a load on his mind'. The work on speedboats undoubtedly eased that load. Lawrence in scruffy overalls with hands stained by oil was the best antidote to the dashing figure in Arab robes with hands stained by guilt. A. W. Lawrence once stated (to many people's

Above: Being based in England he was able to revisit and improve to his best satisfaction his base at Clouds Hill.

'*But my cottage is finished, inside and out, so far as alien hands can finish it – and I feel rooted now, whenever I pass its door. Such a lovely little place, and so plain. It is ingenious, comfortable, bare and restful; and cheap to maintain.*'

Letter to Mrs Charlotte Shaw, May 1934

Left: The upper room at Clouds Hill, dominated in Lawrence's later years by his then state-of-the-art Ginn gramophone. Lawrence acquired a massive collection of classical gramophone records; he was also, as circumstances allowed, an eager visitor to the BBC Promenade Concerts in London.

Right: The lower room, part bedroom, part amazingly well-stocked library.

Below: His earlier Grafonola gramophone, *c.* 1928.

'*Dear Sir Edward*

This is from my cottage, and we have just been playing your 2nd Symphony. Three of us, a sailor, a Tank Corps soldier and myself. So there are all the Services present: and we agreed that you must be written to and told (if you are well enough to be bothered) that this Symphony goes further under our skins than anything else in the record library at Clouds Hill. We have the Violin Concerto, too; so that says quite a lot. Generally we play the Symphony last of all, towards the middle of the night, because nothing comes off very well after it. One seems to stop there.

You would laugh at my cottage, which has one room upstairs (gramophone and records) and one room downstairs (books): but there is also a bath, and we sleep anywhere we feel inclined. So it suits me. A one-man house, I think.'

Letter to Sir Edward Elgar, 22 December 1933:
Elgar died of cancer on 23 February 1934

Left: Lawrence with George Brough, creator of the Brough Superior Motorcycle. A favourite transferable name for his Broughs (he owned seven of them) was 'Boanerges', the New Testament nickname for the disciples James and John, meaning 'Sons of Thunder'.

Top: A small shy man
in mechanic's overalls:
a contrast to the Lawrence
of the public imagination.

Above: Lawrence
photographed with Mrs
Charlotte Shaw, wife of the
playwright Bernard Shaw,
his most constant and most
intimate correspondent
in his later years.

surprise) that even in the overwrought time following his return from the East he had a trick of seeing the funny side of things. Now, after testing the new speed-boats in the Solent and taking them up to Yorkshire, Lawrence could write in a letter to a new literary friend Henry Williamson: 'I'm web-footed now and quack between meals'. To an artist friend he quipped that when he came off duty, since books had not lain much in his way, he was more inclined to read the *Happy Magazine* than Plato: ' So I compromise by reading neither, and am the better mechanic therefor.' Another memorable statement of this time, in a letter to a former wartime colleague, now Lord Lloyd, read: 'After having dabbled in revolt and politics it is rather nice to have been mechanically useful.'

The tense of that last sentence is significant. It was written in September 1934, which meant that the time of his departure from the RAF was rapidly approaching. He had once compared the Air Force to a lay monastery, but this was a monastery that demobilized its monks. On 3 January 1935, from his last posting at Bridlington, he wrote to a Cambridge friend: 'The RAF's solidity and routine have been anchors holding me to life and the world. I wish they had not to be cut.'

On 26 February 1935, in civilian clothes, he bicycled south from Bridlington. His destination was Clouds Hill but over the next few weeks he found himself in a dispiriting struggle to secure the privacy he craved for, going so far as to appeal directly to the Press Association, and even bicycling to Chartwell to enlist the support of his friend Churchill. In effect, all the latter could offer was tea and sympathy, he himself being a man also in the wilderness at that time. When Lawrence did reach Clouds Hill he found himself besieged by pressmen, on one occasion being involved in a fist fight which left him angry and dismayed.

His letters in these final weeks sent mixed signals. The RAF had left 'such a blank afterwards'. There was 'something broken in the works'. 'Sheer bewilderment', was the description of his mood in another letter: 'I imagine leaves must feel like this after they have fallen from the tree and until they die.' In what seems to have been a last letter, he wrote: 'At present I'm sitting in my cottage and getting used to an empty life'; but he added that he was looking forward to the time when this 'spell' is over and 'I begin to go about again'.

'Damn the Press! What line I wish you to take! I wish, like Nero, that the Press had but one neck, and that you would squeeze it. I wish…what do I wish? I wish I were dead, I think. These endings of careers are hurtful things, and I haven't an idea beyond my discharge, and only 25/– [25 shillings] a week, and no courage to take another job, because these news-hounds would smell it out and bay about it. Damn them, as I said. The only way to avoid mention is to join their number, and I'd see them all boiled in paraffin wax first.'

Angry protest: another of his letters to C. P. Robertson
at the Air Ministry, written in early 1935

Above: The final day: Lawrence photographed at Bridlington, Yorkshire, 26 February 1935. on the day he left the RAF, to begin a long slow bicycle journey to Clouds Hill, the main purpose of which was to avoid any publicity. Even in his sanctum at Clouds Hill, journalists pursued him, throwing stones at the cottage roof to bring him out.

Right: View of Clouds Hill, dated 1 May 1935, but possibly taken during the previous month, when Lawrence is known to have been subjected to serious press harassment.

'One of the sorest things in life is to come to realise that one is just not good enough. Better perhaps than some, than many, almost – but I do not care for relatives, for matching against my kind. There is an ideal standard somewhere and only that matters: and I cannot find it. Hence this aimlessness....

Let's come down to earth. You still carve. I still build RAF boats. On March 11th next that office comes to an end. Out I go. Clouds Hill awaits me, as home (address will be Shaw, Clouds Hill, Moreton, Dorset) and I have nearly £2 a week of an income. So I mean to digest all the leisure I can enjoy: and if I find that doing nothing is not worse than this present futile being busy about what doesn't matter – why then, I shall go on doing nothing. But if doing nothing is not good – why then, I shall cut loose again and see where I bring up....'

Letter to Eric Kennington, 6 August 1934

Below and right: The news that shocked the nation in May 1935. His elder brother and mother (seen here in a much later photograph), were en route home from China at the time; on return they immediately set themselves the task of safeguarding his memory.

MR. T. E. SHAW GRAVELY INJURED

MOTORING ACCIDENT IN DORSET

Mr. T. E. Shaw, who recently left the Royal Air Force after serving his engagement as an aircraftman, and who during the War became famous as Colonel T. E. Lawrence, the leader of the Arab irregular forces in the Palestine campaign, was seriously injured yesterday morning through an accident while riding a motorcycle a few miles from Wool, in Dorset. He was removed to the hospital at Bovington Camp, where it was found that his skull was fractured.

Mr. Shaw, since his discharge from the Royal Air Force, has been living in a country cottage at Moreton, in Dorset. Motor-cycling has been his chief recreation.

MAY, 1935

RECORD ON THE ROADS

BIG RISE IN NUMBER OF DEATHS

Nearly 1,000 More Injured

TOTAL OF 4,966

Fatalities 132
Against 112

The road casualties record for Silver Jubilee Week was a particularly bad one.

THE figures published by the Ministry of Transport to-day were:—

Deaths, 132; injured, 4,966.
The figures for the preceding seven days were:—

Deaths, 112; injured, 3,999.
For the week ended 12 May, 1934, the totals were:—

Deaths, 133; injured, 4,565.

Last week's casualties were much the highest since the institution of the 30 m.p.h. speed limit.

It is necessary to go back to 2 February this year to find last week's

"Colonel Lawrence's" Fight For Life

"A Little Weaker, But Holding His Own Well"

MR. T. E. SHAW (otherwise "Lawrence of Arabia") is still unconscious to-day—the third day after a collision with a boy-cyclist near Bovington Camp, Dorset.

If his condition remains unchanged until to-night stronger hopes will be entertained of his ultimate recovery from his serious injury, a fractured skull.

The following bulletin was issued at 10.15 p.m. at the Wool Military Hospital, where he is lying:—

Mr. T. E. Shaw is still in an unconscious condition. He has passed a fair night. His general condition is, if anything, a little weaker, but he is holding his own well.

By that time Mr. Shaw had been unconscious for over 70 hours.

Mr. Shaw's weakness is understood to be due mainly to lack of nourishment owing to his prolonged unconsciousness. He is being artificially fed.

Mr. P. F. Warner,
ENGLAND'S TEST CAPTAIN

Not Even Considered Yet, Says P. F. Warner

Mr. P. F. Warner, chairman of the Cricket Selection Committee, makes the following statement with regard to a report published to-day concerning the captaincy of the England XI. in the forthcoming Test matches against South Africa.

"The Selection Committee has not even considered the question of the captaincy or the composition of the England team.

"As soon as any decision is made it will be announced officially. Mean-

Yet at least he now had his motorcycle re-licensed, considerably more to his liking than his bicycle. However, it was not, it would seem, excessive speed which resulted in the accident which took place on the morning of 13 May 1935. He had gone down on his motorcycle from the cottage to the post office at Bovington Camp, to despatch a parcel to an Air Force friend from Farnborough days and a regular visitor to Clouds Hill, Jock Chambers, and to send a telegram inviting his writer friend Henry Williamson to lunch on the following day. On his way back up the rise leading to Clouds Hill he came upon two errand boys on bicycles and somehow, probably due to nothing more than a simple loss of concentration, managed to clip the wheel of one of them. He fell heavily, and from the head injuries thus received, after lying in a coma in the nearby military hospital for six days, he died, to worldwide shock and mourning, on 19 May, at the age of 46.

PASSING OF "LAWRENCE OF ARABIA"

Tragic End To Brilliant Career

BRAIN DAMAGED IN ACCIDENT

To Be Buried Amid Dorset Hills

FUNERAL AND INQUEST TO-MORROW

"LAWRENCE OF ARABIA," probably the most romantic figure of modern times, died yester-

When War Office Was Surprised

HONOUR REFUSED

Belief That Promises Were Unfulfilled

The real story of Lawrence of Arabia was told yesterday by a man who knew him probably better than any other, a comrade who shared his chief adventures and many of his last hours.

At his own request this man remains anonymous. His story, however, challenged many of the strange legends which have grown around the names of Lawrence of Arabia and Aircraftman Shaw.

"A capable, clever, and forceful man. That is all he was," he said. "To me he was nothing more. All the tales of mystery, intrigue, and espionage are so much fiction. Lawrence had a spirit of revolt in him. In a way he liked to be different. It was this characteristic which caused him to be regarded as a mystery man.

One story of Lawrence which this friend told shows the independence of his spirit. "When he returned from Arabia he was notified by the War Office that he was to be honoured with a decoration from the King. Disappointed at what he believed to be the failure of the Government to fulfil the promises he had made on their behalf, Lawrence replied to the War Office declining the decoration.

A DRAMATIC MEETING

Raising The Arab Standard

AMAZING POWER OF ENDURANCE

LORD LLOYD yesterday gave a "Western Morning News" reporter a graphic story of the entry of Mr. T. E. Shaw (Col. Lawrence) upon his great work among the Arabs during the war.

"The first I ever heard of 'T.E.L.,'" he said, "was in November, 1914, when the little intelligence department in the Old Harbie, Cairo, was being hastily expanded to deal with the situation caused by the entry of the Turks into the war, and their impending attack on the Suez Canal.

"We badly needed an expert on Syria. I well remember 'T. E. L.' unconventionally arriving in Cairo, uniform all awry, and without a Sam Browne belt or military encumbrances of any kind.

"He took charge of the production at

Above: As soon as he was dead the name 'T. E. Shaw' disappeared rapidly from the headlines and he became 'Lawrence of Arabia' again.

Opposite: The generous tribute of his home city's principal newspaper, hailing him as the 'Greatest Oxford Man of his Time'. But there was a dark side to the surge of grief as his life lay in the balance: Clouds Hill had to be put under guard to deter thieves and souvenir-hunters.

Oxford Mail

SPECIAL

No. 2,010. TELEPHONE 4141. SUNDAY, 19 MAY, 1935. 1935. PRICE ONE PENNY.

ENCE OF ARABIA DIES AT BOVIN

SHORTLY AFTER EIGHT O'CLOCK DESPITE SPECIALIS

ON A WAR F THIRTY

Know Who Could at He Did

DISTINCTION

oss and T. E. Shaw gainst Publicity

nd he declined both distinctions.

His work done and Turkish rule over Arabs having been effectively stroyed, Lawrence, with King Felsal, ended the Peace Conference. What happened there is history. His me will live as that of a great glishman who did great work. Allen, after the War, the first counts of Colonel Lawrence's amaz- exploits reached the public and he me world-famous, his extreme ervedness caused him to shrink from sudden publicity and, tiring of ing nothing," he joined the Royal Force under the name of Ross.

TANK CORPS AND R.A.F.

hen his real identity was dis- red he was dismissed as a matter policy " and he joined the Royal Corps as " T. E. Shaw." ter, however, Lawrence was ed to rejoin the R.A.F. 1926 Col. Lawrence published his markable book " Seven Pillars of dom," in which he told for the time the full story of his life ng the Arab tribes. edition was limited to about 100 s, of which a certain number re have been innumerable con- res as to why Lawrence flung and honours aside and buried f in the ranks of the Royal Air

bly the best explanation is to be in his own words. rvice life," he wrote, " teaches a to live largely on little. We g to a big thing which will exist ever and ever in unnumbered ations of standard airmen like es. rmen have no possessions, few little daily care. For me, duty orders only the brightness of fine buttons down my front, every relationship, no loneliness any

reason for not taking a commis- as that he did not mind obeying rders but had an objection

SIR E. FARQHUAR BUZZARD IN CONSULTATION

Oxygen Administered and Doctors Resort to Artificial Respiration in Grim Struggle

GREATEST OXFORD MAN OF HIS TIME

Funeral to be Very Simple With No Wreaths or Flowers

LAWRENCE OF ARABIA

THE " Oxford Mail " deeply regrets to announce that Larence of Arabia is dead. The end came shortly after 8 a.m..

Thus, in a motor cycle accident, perished the greatest mystery figure of modern times, the man who preferred to be known as T. E. Shaw rather than by the name that had become famous, the adventurer who joined the Royal Air Force in order to hide his identity from the public gaze, the glamorous War- time leader on whose head the Turks put the price of £10,000

Thus, too, perishes perhaps the greatest Oxford man of his time. As a boy he was a pupil of the Oxford High School. Later he went to Jesus College and was elected to a Demy- ship of Magdalen.

The distinguished Oxford physcian, Sir E. Farquhar Buzzard, had been called into consultation. But all was of no avail. Lawrence of Arabia died at the age of 46 in the Military Hospital of Bovington Camp, Dorset.

BROTHER'S CEASELESS VIGIL

For 106 hours Lawrence had lain unconscious, following the collision between his motor-cycle and a boy cyclist near the military camp, and near the cottage which the ex-AirCraft- man was preparing for his own retirement.

Throughout that time his brother, Mr. A. W. Lawrence, and his friend and servant, Pat Knowles, had maintained a ceaseless vigil, while famous specialists t ried to have his life.

It was realised yesterday that the crisis had been reached. Sir Farquhar Buzard, Physician in Ordinary to the King, and probably the greatest living authority on Neurology, was called in. Mr. H. W. B. Caird, the brain specialist, and D. H.

M. Laval To Visit Germany?

Lunch With Gen. Goering and M. Beck

GEN. GOERING (the German Air Minister), M. Laval (the French Foreign Minister) and Col

PUPIL OF T HIGH S

Later Demy of Mag Fellow of

" COL. LAWRENCE " was in- timately associated with Ox- ford.

Born in Wales, he came as a boy of eight to live with his parents in a house in Polstead-road, Oxford.

He went to Oxford High School, as it was then called, where he remained for 11 years.

It was there that he developed his strong interest in archaeology. He spent a great part of his holidays either ex- ploring or watching where excava- tions were in progress to see what he could carry off and prepare for the Ashmolean Museum.

SCHOOLBOY EXPLOITS

Although unpopular because of his contempt for games, he became the hero of the school when he negotiated the Trill Mill stream which runs for about a mile under the City, from the Castle to near Folly Bridge.

Another of his exploits, which few have attempted, was the navigation of the Cherwell from Banbury to Oxford in a canoe.

In one of the eddies Lawrence was thrown out, and after swimming ashore to dry his clothes in the sun, he sat in the canoe in a rug.

From the High School, Lawrence went to Jesus College; he was elected to a Senior Demyship at Magdalen in 1911.

ENTRY INTO ASIA

Before he finished his course at Oxford he went to Asia Minor, Syria and Palestine. No sooner had he arrived than he adopted native costume and tramped over thousands of miles of unknown desert country, living with tribes and studying their manners and customs.

His outstanding taste at that period was still for archaeology, and he was engaged from 1910 until the outbreak of war in the excavations which were being carried out under the auspices of the British Museum on the Euphrates.

It was during these years that he came to know the Bedouins better than most people.

Then came the War. His earliest effort to join the Army was in 1914. Only 5ft. 3in. tall, this studious, shy young man came before the doctors, who turned him down as physically unfit and advised him to " run home to his mother and wait for the next war."

For some time after his rejection he returned to the ruins of Asia

right column partial:
M
H
O

cord 29.5

The a dis flowe destro

But cast, Oxf degre minin month ing vious it bea war.

The pall-bearers at Lawrence's funeral in Moreton, Dorset, 21 May 1935; Arnold Lawrence and his wife Barbara (not shown) followed immediately behind the bier.

The funeral took place at Moreton, just across the heath from Clouds Hill, two days later. There was an appropriate mix of mourners. It included Mr and Mrs Winston Churchill, Lord Lloyd, Lady Astor, General Wavell, Augustus John, and Siegfried Sassoon. The pall-bearers were Sir Ronald Storrs, Colonel Newcombe, Eric Kennington, Corporal Bradbury of the RAF, Arthur Russell of the Tank Corps, and Lawrence's neighbour and aide at Clouds Hill, Pat Knowles. The interment took place not in the churchyard proper but in a small graveyard several hundred yards down the road.

Lawrence's youngest brother, Arnold, was the only member of the family present, his mother and elder brother being on the way back from their missionary activities in China. They would make their contribution to the event retrospectively, when Kennington was commissioned to carve Lawrence's headstone. The only attribution included was 'Fellow of All Souls College Oxford', while much of the remaining space was filled by a verse from St John's Gospel, Chapter 5: 'The hour is coming & now is when the dead shall hear the voice of the Son of God and they that hear shall live.' There is, perhaps, an understandable explanation of both inscriptions: arguably the first shows the pride of a family which had come to Oxford under a shadow and could now boast a member who had achieved one of the university's most honoured accolades; while the second reveals his mother's constant hope that her sons might help her to atone for her sins by becoming fervent warriors of the Christian faith. Bob had lived up to her dream, Arnold would reject her creed entirely, while for his part T. E. never quite resolved the matter of belief and unbelief. As in so many other respects he remains a man who raises unanswerable questions. Yet this was also the man of whom John Buchan said that he could follow him over the edge of the world, and of whom Eric Kennington's wife, Celandine, said that 'he lit so many fires in cold rooms'.

'We shall never see his like again… His name will live in history. It will live in the annals of war – it will live in the legends of Arabia.'

Winston Churchill

Left: The mourners, most prominent among them Mr and Mrs Winston Churchill. Also present were Lady Astor, Siegfried Sassoon, Augustus John, Lord Lloyd, General Wavell, Lionel Curtis and Mrs Thomas Hardy. The simple funeral included one psalm, one hymn, prayers and the *Nunc Dimittis*. There was no funeral oration.

Above: Lawrence's grave in the cemetery extension at Moreton. The inscription, chosen by his mother and elder brother, reflected religious convictions which Lawrence himself had largely discarded.

THE LEGEND AND THE LEGACY

ENVOI

'Lawrence of Arabia':
The frequently reproduced
classic portrait by Augustus
John, 1919. The original is
in the Tate Britain, London.
A copy is held at Jesus
College, Oxford.

'**As for fame-after-death**, it's a thing to spit at; the only minds worth winning are the warm ones about us. If we miss those we are failures.'

Lawrence wrote those words, in a letter to the publisher Peter Davies, on 25 February 1935, just under twelve weeks before he died. Fame after death was inevitable in his case and the ripples of his fame have been widening ever since.

First there was a spontaneous surge of grief, and not only in Britain, for he was by now an internationally known figure and the shock of his death was felt virtually worldwide. One whose distress was so movingly expressed that David Garnett later gave it pride of place in his 1951 collection *The Essential T. E. Lawrence* was Sheikh Hamoudi, foreman at Carchemish and friend of Dahoum, with whom he had visited the Lawrence family in Oxford back in 1913. 'Told of T. E. Lawrence's death', wrote Garnett, 'Hamoudi strode up and down a stone-flagged hall in Aleppo exclaiming in his grief: "Oh! If only he had died in battle! I have lost my son, but I do not grieve for him as I do for Lawrence... I am counted brave, the bravest of my tribe; my heart was iron, but his was steel. A man whose hand was never closed, but open... Tell them... Tell them in England what I say. Of manhood the man, in freedom free; a mind without equal; I can see no flaw in him.'"

Soon the memorialization of Lawrence began. On 29 January 1936 a bust of him by Eric Kennington, made some years earlier, was unveiled in St Paul's Cathedral, London. The speaker who delivered the address was one of the nation's highest luminaries, Lord Halifax, former Viceroy of India, Chancellor of Oxford University, future Foreign Secretary and Ambassador to the United States, though another qualification for his presence was that he had served as Parliamentary Under-Secretary for the Colonies when Lawrence was attached to the Colonial Office in 1921–22. His tribute to Lawrence was fulsome, striking the kind of note that would virtually guarantee an ultimate reaction against him. There were references to Lawrence's 'almost mesmeric power', to 'his mastery over life', to 'the consuming fire that made him so different from the common run of men'. One paragraph almost interpreted him as a figure of ancient myth:

Strange how he loved the naked places of the earth, which seemed to match the austerity of life as he thought that it should be lived. And so he loved the desert where wide spaces are lost in distance, and, wanderer himself, found natural kinship with the wandering peoples of his adopted home.

A cast of the bust was subsequently installed in the chapel of Jesus College, Oxford. But already Kennington had begun working on his finest image of Lawrence, the recumbent effigy depicting him in Arab clothes that would be placed in the tiny church of St Martin's Wareham in 1939. Later, in 1954 a cement cast would be made, to be reworked by the sculptor and held in the Tate Gallery, London, now known as Tate Britain.

Meanwhile his inevitable celebration in print had begun. Despite what was denounced as a 'perverse cult' by some owners of the subscribers' edition who held that *Seven Pillars of Wisdom* should be denied to the general public, Lawrence's seminal work soon appeared in the bookshops, to instant acclaim. It would become a publishing phenomenon, would never be off the shelves and would be issued in numerous formats and as many as seventeen languages.

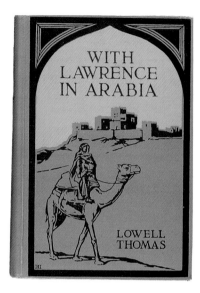

Above: Lowell Thomas's best-seller, based on his lectures, the first American edition, New York 1924, claiming to tell 'the greatest story to come out of the war.' By the outbreak of the Second World War the book had sold almost 200,000 copies in Britain.

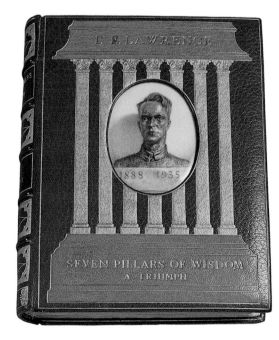

Right: Lawrence by Augustus John, also, like the portrait on page 186, painted in 1919. Lawrence called that portrait the 'wrathful' one, while describing this as the 'goody-goody one'. Another iconic image, it is held in the United States at Yale University's Center for British Art.

Opposite: *Seven Pillars of Wisdom*. The first public edition, 1935, in a special 'Cosway' binding produced by the London booksellers Henry Sotheran, with a miniature portrait of the author by Miss Currie. On sale ten weeks after his death, the book was an instant success, with 60,000 copies ordered before publication. It has never since been out of print.

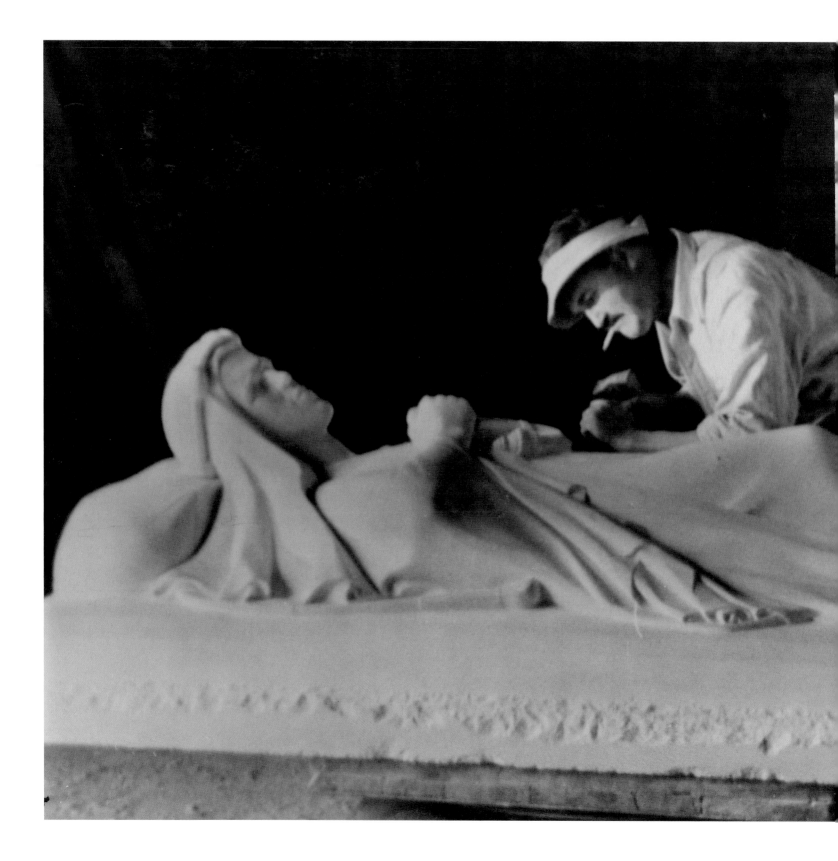

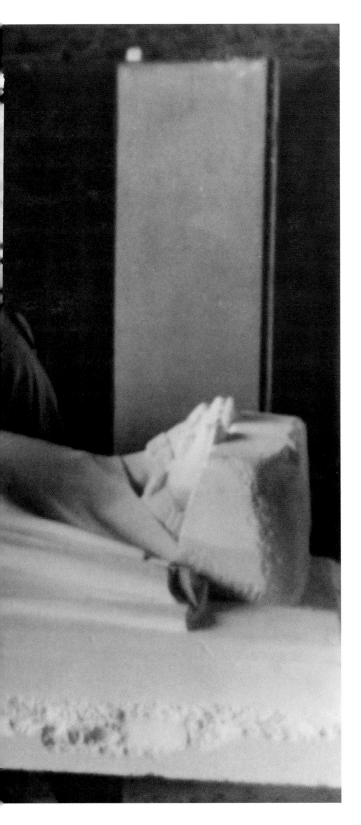

Realizing this had started a surge of interest which one book alone could not satisfy, his brother, A.W. Lawrence, began compiling a substantial volume of reminiscences, which appeared in 1937 under the title of *T. E. Lawrence by his Friends*. Some of Lawrence's closest associates, including Feisal and Hogarth, had died, but nevertheless almost eighty contributors responded to his brother's invitation, from such high-profile figures as Winston Churchill, Bernard Shaw, E. M. Forster and Robert Graves to colleagues from his school and university days and former comrades in the Royal Air Force and Tank Corps. Lord Halifax's speech at St Paul's in the previous year was incorporated as the book's Introduction.

Back in 1929 Lawrence had written to an RAF friend: 'I am trying to accustom myself to the truth that probably I'll be talked over for the rest of my life: and after my life, too. There will be a volume of "letters" after I die.' This prediction became doubly true in 1938, when a rich collection almost 900 pages long, entitled *The Letters of T. E. Lawrence*, edited by David Garnett with scrupulous scholarship, and with the extra element of the affection of an admiring friend, was published, to general satisfaction and acclaim. Subsequently in 1939 the Golden Cockerel Press, a leading name among small high-quality presses at that time, published a limited edition of his wartime reports under the title of *Secret Despatches from Arabia*. Being still officially under legal embargo, their appearance in public print required a special dispensation from the British Foreign Office. The dispensation was granted without demur.

Right: Lawrence's headcloth, open and boxed and a robe said to have been given to him by Feisal.

Below: Gold dagger, made for Lawrence in Mecca in 1917: as worn in the photographs on pages 34 and 149.

Right: A modern 'relic': a specially commissioned carving, based on Lawrence's 'Hittite' carving at Carchemish (see page 26).

Opposite: Augustus John, pencil drawing (detail),1919

This was the beginning of a whole literature that would eventually embrace so many works, books of various genres, plays, film-scripts, articles, dissertations, and more – including a glut of biographies and novels for children – that the latest edition of a Lawrence bibliography compiled by the distinguished American scholar Philip O'Brien is almost exactly as long as David Garnett's volume of letters, 894 pages to Garnett's 896.

The Second World War took Lawrence out of public notice, but he was not forgotten. There were generals of more than one nation who knew and appreciated his military insights, including the German Erwin Rommel and the American George S. Patton, while Churchill as Prime Minister and war leader was always on the look-out for commanders of Lawrence's calibre. He found one in Orde Wingate, described by his private secretary John Martin 'as an interesting and striking person, not unlike my idea of T. E. Lawrence.' Wingate himself, it should be said, was not a personal admirer of Lawrence, yet the tactics he employed won him such unwelcome nicknames as the Lawrence of Judea (for his activities in Palestine) and, later, the Lawrence of Burma. When the Royal Central Asian Society recognized Wingate's achievements, they awarded him the Lawrence of Arabia memorial medal.

It could not last. If not *his* hubris, that of those who uncritically saw him as an unassailable historic figure was almost bound to invite chastisement. The savagely critical biography by Richard Aldington published in 1955 rocked his reputation like an explosive charge attached to a statue. It can, however, be claimed that Aldington's debunking attack ultimately proved salutary, in that, by opening the subject to serious scholarly inquiry, it helped to create the fairer equilibrium which prevails today.

Ironically, that this would happen was foreseen by one of the most notable contributors to *T. E. Lawrence by his Friends*, Major-General A. P. Wavell, who had written in a perceptive passage: 'He will always have his detractors, those who sneer at the "Lawrence legend"; those who ascribe his success with the Arabs to gold; who view the man as a charlatan in search of notoriety by seeming to seek obscurity; who regard his descent from colonel to private as evidence of some morbid *nostalgie de la boue*. They knew not the man.'

'He will always have his detractors, those who sneer at the "Lawrence legend"; those who ascribe his successes with the Arabs to gold; who view the man as a charlatan in search of notoriety by seeming to seek obscurity; who regard his descent from colonel to private as evidence of some morbid nostalgie de la boue. *They knew not the man.'*

Major-General A. P. Wavell

Last month in uniform: charcoal sketch by Augustus John, January 1935.

Strangely, 'the man' would also be as much distorted as rehabilitated by the next major development in the propagation of the Lawrence saga: the highly popular, Oscar-winning movie *Lawrence of Arabia*, directed by David Lean and with Peter O'Toole in the title role, which premiered in 1962 and exported his wartime exploits around the world, bringing in a whole new generation of *aficionados*. It also inspired a new, and continuing, wave of biographies pro and con. Much of it re-staged in the actual desert locations, it was a magnificent piece of film-making, though – understandably, since this was a feature film not a documentary – in numerous respects more Hollywood than history. The character of the central figure, as flamboyantly though brilliantly portrayed by O'Toole (who apart from anything else was almost a foot taller than the original), dismayed and enraged many of Lawrence's friends.

Yet in the end it is 'the man', the real person under the glamour and the gloss, the adulation on the one hand and the denigration on the other, who now fascinates, while the camel-mounted figure of the desert war increasingly takes second place. It is the less colourful, more earthbound Lawrence of the final years who catches the greater interest, a Lawrence for whom many people feel something approaching a personal rapport: the man struggling with the positive and negative aspects of his own complex personality, with his motives, his beliefs, his sexuality, the man facing the question as to what to do with a career the highest moments of which were so soon over, leaving him with shadows from which he could never escape as long as he lived. A substantial part of his legacy, in short, is not in his achievements and his successes but in his humanity and his vulnerability, in the manner in which he tackles the problem of living, in the ways in which he is or seems like us.

Yet Lawrence also left behind a different, more objective legacy, a literary and visual one, a cultural cornucopia, some fragments of which have been gathered together to create this book.

However, this is not how this narrative should end. The changing world of the new century requires a new assessment of one aspect, indeed, in the context of his reputation as 'Lawrence of Arabia', the

Left: William Roberts' admiration for Lawrence persisted long after the latter's death. Hence this remarkable painting, entitled *Revolt in the Desert*, dating from 1954. Lawrence – his identity made clear by his dagger – is depicted bottom right, accompanied by a party of Bedouin tribesmen, some on foot, some on camels. Originally of the Vorticist school, by this time Roberts had developed his own highly idiosyncratic style.

Opposite: This equally strange painting, simply entitled *T. E. Lawrence*, dates from twenty years earlier, 1934. By an Austrian-born religious artist named Herbert Gurschner, it was commissioned by a distant relative of Lawrence on his father's side for a book that was never published. Almost certainly based on photographs, there being no evidence of any sittings. After his brother's death, Arnold Lawrence was approached by numerous admirers who had seen T. E. as the central figure of a religion, and who saw him, Arnold, as its potential St Paul. 'I had, I should think, something like 500 letters ...the majority wanted me to take up his mantle.' Gurschner's interpretation catches such attitudes with uncanny accuracy.

prime aspect, of this man's chequered, indeed meteoric, career. A minor figure in the war which gave him the opportunity (to quote his own words) 'to write [his] will across the sky in stars', he has now become a major figure in the context of the insurgency wars, the anti-terrorism conflicts, which have taken over from the Cold War as the major threat to the peace and stability of the world. In this area, where such First World War luminaries as Foch, Ludendorff, Hindenburg, Haig or Pershing have nothing to contribute, the eloquent, maverick liaison officer to Feisal in his 'sideshow of a sideshow' has suddenly emerged as a figure of considerable importance. Historians and commentators have begun quoting him as an authority with something relevant to say about the new warfare of the Middle East, which is now even more the world's crucible than it was in his day. Thus the man from whose writings the compilers of the *Oxford Dictionary of Modern Quotations* could find only three statements they deemed worth including is being quoted again and again almost as though he were the author of a newly discovered gospel. Launching what has become a major stream of powerful invective and argument, *The Times* of London, in March 2004, printed an article entitled 'Lawrence of

O'Toole of Arabia

Opposite: Scenes from the famous feature film which turned Lawrence's story into a box-office phenomenon and won a spate of Oscars. Peter O'Toole became a superstar through his brilliant portrayal of the central role, but many who had known the man saw the film as a travesty.

Right: One of numerous posters advertising the 1962 feature film, itself the realization of an ambition conceived by Alexander Korda in the 1930s.

From the creators of "The Bridge On The River Kwai."
Columbia Pictures presents The SAM SPIEGEL · DAVID LEAN Production of

LAWRENCE OF ARABIA

"I deem him one of the greatest beings alive in our time. ...we shall never see his like again. His name will live in history. It will live in the annals of war...It will live in the legends of Arabia!"
—WINSTON CHURCHILL

ALEC GUINNESS · ANTHONY QUINN
JACK HAWKINS · JOSE FERRER
ANTHONY QUAYLE · CLAUDE RAINS · ARTHUR KENNEDY
PETER O'TOOLE as LAWRENCE · OMAR SHARIF as ALI
ROBERT BOLT · SAM SPIEGEL · DAVID LEAN · TECHNICOLOR®
SUPER PANAVISION 70°

Arabia's lessons on the Iraq war', with, under a subtitle headed 'The Wisdom of T. E. Lawrence', a clutch of notable sayings:

¶ *'Armies are like plants, immobile, firm-rooted, nourished through long stems to the head. Guerrillas are like a vapour.'*

¶ *Of the Turks: 'War upon rebellion was messy and slow, like eating soup with a knife.'*

¶ *To lead guerrilla fighters you must be one of them. 'They taught me that no man could be their leader except he ate the ranks' food, wore their clothes, lived with them and yet appeared better in himself.'*

¶ *The power of hope and imagination makes men dangerous. 'All men dream: but not equally. Those who dream by night in the dusty recesses of their minds wake in the day to find that it was vanity: but the dreamers of the day are dangerous men, for they may act their dream with open eyes, to make it possible.'*

The newspaper reported a massive surge in sales of *Seven Pillars of Wisdom* and, in a leading article, stated that what was 'truly invaluable' about Lawrence's approach was his determination 'to understand the Arab mindset' and that his genius was in the pains he took to do so. 'A military officer steeped in Lawrence's respect for Arab ways … will do a far better job of winning hearts and minds than one who comes to the job with no specialist knowledge.' Simultaneously the cause was taken up robustly in the United States, where Lawrence has become required reading in the military hierarchy as well as a subject of serious and lengthy discussion in the nation's leading newspapers. So now there is another element to be added to the legacy of this extraordinary man. Dying seventy years before the publication of this book, and of numerous others picking over his remarkable career, T. E. Lawrence has shown that he still has power to fascinate and astonish, and also, in areas where his knowledge and experience were second to none, to inform and instruct. His story is far from over.

Bust of Lawrence by Eric Kennington. The original is in St Paul's Cathedral, London, reflecting his national fame. A cast is held in the chapel of Jesus College, Oxford, reflecting his modest scholarly origins.

Cast of Characters

ABDULLAH IBN HUSSEIN (1882–1951)
Abdullah was the second son of Hussein ibn Ali, Grand Sherif of Mecca. Lawrence met Abdullah in October 1916 and although he judged him to be an astute politician, he decided that he was not the man to lead the Arab Revolt. While this role fell to his younger brother Feisal, Abdullah served as his father's foreign minister. Abdullah later became Emir (and subsequently King) of Transjordan until his assassination in Jerusalem in 1951, when he was succeeded by his grandson, King Hussein, a central figure in Middle Eastern politics until his death in 1999.

GENERAL SIR EDMUND ALLENBY, LATER FIRST VISCOUNT ALLENBY OF MEGIDDO (1861–1936)
Allenby's career in the British Army began in South Africa. He went to France with the British Expeditionary Force in 1914 as G.O.C. (General Officer Commanding) of the Cavalry Division. In 1915 he was given command of the Third Army, but following a less than convincing performance in April 1917 at the Battle of Arras, in June that year he was appointed Commander-in-Chief of the Egyptian Expeditionary Force in the Middle East. He succeeded Sir Archibald Murray, who had twice failed in attacks on Gaza. In marked contrast to his predecessor, he revived the morale of the EEF, took Gaza, and in December 1917 captured Jerusalem. In September 1918, he launched a major offensive against the Turks which led to the capture of Damascus. His influence on Lawrence was profound; despite differences in their personalities, the two men achieved a mutual respect, each recognizing the contribution the other made to the overall objectives of the campaign. Ennobled after the war, he served as special high commissioner in Egypt from 1919 until his retirement in 1925.

AUDA ABU TAYI (c. 1870–1924)
Auda Abu Tayi, sheikh of the Abu Tayi Bedouin, a branch of the Howeitat based in the area around Maan, was one of the fiercest warriors in the region, whose support was considered essential for the success of the Arab Revolt. He was repeatedly approached by the Turks with financial inducements if he would switch to their side, but refused to go back on his word. He reputedly married 28 times and was wounded more than a dozen times in action. Legend had it that he had killed 75 Arabs by his own hand; he did not keep count of the number of Turks. He and his tribesmen played a major part in the capture of Akaba and he was with Lawrence at the entry into Damascus. After the war, Auda returned to his home town of El-Jefer to build himself a great *kasr* (palace) of mud-brick using Turkish prisoner-labour. However, a lifetime of hard riding and hard fighting finally caught up with him, and he died in 1924 while still in his mid-fifties.

DAHOUM (SELIM OR SHEIKH AHMED) (1896–1918)
Dahoum was employed as one of the donkey boys at the Carchemish site, where he met Lawrence in 1911 and tended him while he was ill. Lawrence employed Dahoum as a personal servant and encouraged him in his efforts to learn to read and write. He took Dahoum along with Sheikh Hamoudi, the site foreman, on a visit to Oxford in July 1913, and Dahoum accompanied Lawrence, Woolley and Newcombe on the expedition to the Sinai Desert in early 1914. Dahoum died of fever some time during the war, although Lawrence may not have learned of his death until 1918. He has generally but certainly been identified as the 'S.A.' to whom *Seven Pillars of Wisdom* is dedicated.

FAREEDEH EL AKLE (1892–1976)
Fareedeh el Akle was a Syrian, a Christian and an Arab nationalist. Lawrence first met her in 1909 when she was teaching at the American Mission School at Jebail, and he studied Arabic with her in 1911. Lawrence later sought her advice when he was teaching Dahoum to read, and they continued to correspond until 1927. Lost to view for many years, she made a notable contribution to a BBC documentary on Lawrence in 1962.

FEISAL IBN HUSSEIN (1886–1933)
Lawrence, who first encountered Feisal, the third son of Hussein ibn Ali, in October 1916, saw him as the best qualified of the three sons he had met to lead the Arab Revolt. Adept at settling tribal disputes, Feisal held together the Arab forces during the course of the war and emerged as the chief negotiator for the Arab cause (with Lawrence as adviser) at the Paris Peace Conference. In March 1920 he proclaimed himself King of Syria and Palestine, but was expelled by the French in July. Following the Cairo Conference of 1921 he was nominated by the British for the throne of Iraq, where he reigned as king from 1921 until his death in 1933 at the age of 48. The brutal removal of the regime he founded by the Baathist party in 1958 ultimately led to the dictatorship of Saddam Hussein, who was deposed by American and British intervention in 2003.

DAVID GEORGE HOGARTH (1862–1927)
D. G. Hogarth was an eminent scholar, archaeologist and traveller, who in 1908 became Keeper of the Ashmolean Museum in Oxford, where he met the undergraduate Lawrence. He recommended Lawrence for a demyship (senior scholarship) at Magdalen, his own college, invited him to take part in the excavations at Carchemish, and encouraged him to learn Arabic. During the early part of the war Hogarth worked with Lawrence in the Arab Bureau in Cairo and afterwards at the Paris Peace Conference. He was, perhaps, the person Lawrence most respected and his death left Lawrence with a deep sense of personal bereavement.

HUSSEIN IBN ALI, GRAND SHERIF HUSSEIN (1853–1931)
Hussein became Emir (or Grand Sherif) of Mecca in 1908. While maintaining his position with Turkey he negotiated with Sir Henry McMahon during 1915–16 the terms of the Arab revolt against the Turkish Empire. At the beginning of the revolt he proclaimed himself 'king of the Arab lands' while Britain simply recognized him as 'king of the Hejaz'. The settlements after the war, which benefited his sons Feisal and Abdullah, left Hussein isolated, and in 1925 he abdicated in favour of his eldest son Ali. Within months Ali had been defeated by the Wahabi leader Ibn Sa'ud, who founded the modern kingdom of Saudi Arabia. Hussein was exiled to Cyprus but achieved his ambition to end his days on Islamic soil, dying in Amman, Jordan, in 1931. He was buried in Jerusalem on the Dome of the Rock.

ERIC HENRI KENNINGTON (1888–1960)

Eric Kennington worked as an artist in London before the First World War. He fought in France and Flanders, but was wounded and became an official war artist. Lawrence admired his work, and appointed him as art editor for *Seven Pillars of Wisdom*. In 1921 Kennington travelled to the Middle East and drew a series of striking pastel portraits of Arab leaders. Kennington's interest later turned towards sculpture, and he carved the effigy of Lawrence now in St Martin's Church in Wareham, Dorset.

ARNOLD WALTER LAWRENCE (1900–91)

A. W. Lawrence ('Arnie'), the youngest of T. E. Lawrence's brothers, attended the City of Oxford School and New College, Oxford. Afterwards, he studied as an archaeologist in Rome and Athens and worked with Leonard Woolley at Ur. He held academic posts in Cambridge and later was professor of archaelogy at the University College of Ghana and director of the Ghana National Museum. After his brother's death in 1935, A. W. Lawrence became his literary executor and effectively the defender of his reputation against those who attacked it in print or misrepresented it (in his view) on film. A man of distinct intellectual rigour, he did not suffer sycophants gladly, but was prepared to help and advise those who came to him with serious scholarly intent.

MONTAGU ROBERT LAWRENCE (1885–1971)

'Bob', the eldest of Lawrence's brothers, was born in Dublin and educated at the City of Oxford High School and St John's College, Oxford. He qualified as a doctor and served with the Royal Army Medical Corps during the war. In 1921 he joined the China Inland Mission and in 1935 was en route home from China with their mother Sarah Lawrence when T. E. had his fatal accident. He later edited *The Home Letters of T. E. Lawrence and His Brothers*, published in 1954.

STEWART FRANCIS NEWCOMBE (1878–1956)

Stewart Newcombe was a captain in the Royal Engineers when he was asked to conduct a military survey of the Sinai peninsula in November 1913. He was assisted by Lawrence and Woolley, who were there ostensibly to record the archaeological sites. During the early part of the Arab Revolt he was effectively Lawrence's commanding officer, being appointed head of the British Military mission in the Hejaz in January 1917. However, his capture in November by the Turks near Beersheba ended his part in the campaign. In 1920 he named his son Stewart Lawrence Newcombe in honour of his wartime colleague and friend. He was one of the pallbearers at Lawrence's funeral.

MRS CHARLOTTE SHAW (1857–1943)

Charlotte Frances Payne-Townshend was born in Dublin to a wealthy Irish family. She became a friend of Sidney and Beatrice Webb, and through them met the rising Irish playwright George Bernard Shaw (1856–1950) whom she married in 1898. Lawrence was introduced to the Shaws in 1922, and became, especially to Charlotte, almost a surrogate son. Their correspondence extended over the rest of Lawrence's life and covered a wide range of literary and other cultural subjects as well as aspects of Lawrence's personal life that he seldom discussed with others.

SYDNEY WILLIAM SMITH (1888–1971)

Having obtained his pilot's licence in 1913, in 1914 Sydney Smith was seconded to the Royal Flying Corps (later merged with the Royal Naval Air Service into the Royal Air Force) and served in France until 1916. He met Lawrence at the Cairo Conference in 1921 and again at RAF Cranwell in 1926. In 1929, on Lawrence's return from India, Wing Commander Smith became his commanding officer at RAF Mount Batten, Plymouth. Lawrence was on friendly terms with Smith and with his wife Clare, who later wrote a moving account of this period, published in 1940 as *The Golden Reign*. Smith moved to RAF Manston in 1931 and subsequently served in the Far East. He was awarded the OBE (Officer of the Order of the British Empire) for his services, and retired with the rank of Air Commodore.

SIR RONALD STORRS (1881–1955)

Ronald Storrs studied Classics and Arabic at Cambridge, and in 1909 became Oriental Secretary to the administration based in Cairo, where he had considerable influence on British policy in the Middle East. Storrs first met Lawrence in Cairo in 1915, when both were members of the Arab Bureau, and he took Lawrence with him to Jidda and Rabegh in October 1916. Following the capture of Jerusalem in 1917, Storrs became its Military (later Civil) Governor. After the war he served as Governor of Cyprus and of Northern Rhodesia. He was a pallbearer at Lawrence's funeral.

LOWELL JACKSON THOMAS (1892–1981)

The journalist and publicist Lowell Thomas was sent to Europe with his photographer, Harry Chase, with a view to increasing popular support for the war effort in America. Having found little material on the Western Front, they travelled to the Middle East, where Thomas first met Lawrence in Jerusalem in the spring of 1918. They later spent a couple of weeks with Lawrence in Akaba. The material he and Chase gathered formed the basis of Thomas's illustrated travelogues which turned Lawrence into an international celebrity. Lawrence was both repelled and fascinated by Thomas's romanticized presentation of his exploits. In 1924, Thomas published *With Lawrence in Arabia* and subsequently wrote a children's book on the same subject. Later Thomas became a commentator on world events for 20th Century Fox Movietone and NBC in America.

SIR (CHARLES) LEONARD WOOLLEY (1880–1960)

Leonard Woolley's interest in archaeology developed while he was studying at Oxford, and in 1905 he was appointed assistant to the Keeper of the Ashmolean Museum, He took charge of the excavations at Carchemish for the second season (1912–13), where Lawrence, whom he already knew slightly, was his assistant. In 1914 Woolley, Lawrence and Newcombe carried out the military survey of Sinai, published as *The Wilderness of Zin*. After the war, during which Woolley was captured by the Turks, he became famous for his excavations at Ur in southern Iraq.

Chronology

1888

16 August: born at Tremadoc, North Wales, the second of five illegitimate sons born to Mr and Mrs T. R. Lawrence, formerly Thomas Robert Tighe Chapman and Sarah, surname uncertain, former governess to Chapman's four daughters by his legitimate wife, Edith; the marriage was never dissolved.

1896

The family settles in Oxford.

1896–1907

At City of Oxford High School. In France, studying castles, summers of 1906 and 1907.

1907–10

October 1907–June 1910: at Jesus College, Oxford. Summer 1908: in France, studying castles. Summer 1909: in Syria, studying crusader castles. Winter 1909–10: works on thesis on crusader castles. Summer 1910: 1st Class Honours in Modern History.

1910

Travels to the Middle East; winter at Jebail, Lebanon, learning Arabic.

1911

February–March: travels to Carchemish. April–July: excavating at Carchemish under D. G. Hogarth and R. Campbell Thompson. Summer: walk through northern Mesopotamia.

1912

January: in Egypt excavating under Flinders Petrie.

1912–14

Spring 1912–Spring 1914: excavating at Carchemish under C. L. Woolley.

Summer 1913: at home in Oxford, with Hamoudi and Dahoum. January–February 1914: Sinai survey with Woolley and Captain Newcombe.

1914

Summer: at Oxford and London, completing *The Wilderness of Zin* (archaeological report on Sinai co-written with Woolley). October: joined War Office (geographical division of Military Intelligence). 26 October: commissioned as Second Lieutenant on the Special List (i.e. without regimental attachment).

1914–16

December 1914–October 1916: in Egypt as Intelligence Officer. March–May 1916: on special duty in Mesopotamia.

1916

5 June: Arab Revolt begins. 16 October: arrives in Arabia as part of a British military mission. 23 October: first meeting with Feisal. November: joins Arab Bureau. December 1916–October 1918: attached as liaison officer to Arab forces.

1917

8 January: Feisal's army leaves Yenbo en route for Wejh, arriving 25 January. 9 May: start of Akaba expedition under Sherif Nasir. June: Lawrence's northern journey. 6 July: seizure of Akaba. July: Lawrence's first meeting with General Sir Edmund Allenby. Promoted to Major. October–November: unsuccessful raid in Yarmuk Valley. 20 November: capture and rape at Deraa. 11 December: Lawrence present at Allenby's entry into Jerusalem.

1918

15 January: Battle of Tafileh. March: promoted to Lieutenant-Colonel. Joint actions by Allenby's and Arab Forces postponed because of pressing need for troops in France following launch of major German offensive. Spring–Summer: raids continue. 19 September: Allenby launches offensive against Turkish forces in Palestine with Feisal's Arabs acting as right wing in the desert. 1 October: arrival at Damascus. 4 October: departure of Lawrence for Cairo and London. October–November: Lawrence present at Eastern Committee of War Cabinet. November–December: with Feisal in France and Britain.

1919

January–October: in Paris for Peace Conference. May–June: journey by air to Egypt.

1919–21

At All Souls College, Oxford (elected as Fellow, November 1918), in Paris and London, working on *Seven Pillars of Wisdom*. August: Lowell Thomas's Middle Eastern entertainment opens in London.

1921–22

Adviser to Winston Churchill at the Colonial Office. August–December 1921: missions to Aden, Jidda and Transjordan. July 1922: resigns from Colonial Office.

1922

August: joins Royal Air Force as John Hume Ross, sent to RAF training depot, Uxbridge. November: transferred to RAF School of Photography, Farnborough. 27 December: discovered by the press.

1923

January: discharged following disclosure of his identity.

1923–25

March 1923–August 1925: serves in the Army as Private T. E. Shaw, Royal Tank Corps. Summer 1923: acquires cottage at Clouds Hill, near Bovington Camp, Dorset.

1925

18 August: rejoins the Royal Air Force as Aircraftman T. E. Shaw; sent to RAF Cranwell, Lincolnshire.

1926

Subscribers' edition of *Seven Pillars of Wisdom* completed.

1927–29

January 1927–January 1929: in India; *Revolt in the Desert* (popular abridgement of *Seven Pillars*) published, later withdrawn; *The Mint* completed; work begun on translation of *Odyssey*; formally adopts the surname Shaw by deed poll. December 1929: ordered home by Air Ministry following press stories claiming his involvement in a rebellion in Afghanistan.

1929–35

At various air stations in England, working with Sydney Smith on Schneider Trophy, September 1929, subsequently on high-speed marine craft. Final base, Bridlington, Yorkshire.

1935

26 February: Lawrence leaves Royal Air Force, with a view to retirement at Clouds Hill. 13 May: has accident on motorcycle near Clouds Hill. 19 May: dies in Bovington Military Hospital. 21 May: funeral at Moreton, Dorset.

Further Reading

T. E. Lawrence, *Seven Pillars of Wisdom: A Triumph*, Harmondsworth, Penguin Books; New York, Doubleday (constantly in print)

T. E. Lawrence, *Seven Pillars of Wisdom: A Triumph*, 1922 (Oxford) Version, Fordingbridge, Hants, Castle Hill Press, 1997

T. E. Lawrence, *The Mint*, Harmondsworth, Penguin Books; New York, Doubleday (constantly in print)

T. E. Lawrence, *Oriental Assembly*, London, Williams & Norgate, 1939; New York, Dutton, 1940; London, Imperial War Museum, 1991, 2005

David Garnett (editor), *The Letters of T. E. Lawrence*, London, Jonathan Cape, 1938; New York, Doubleday, Doran, 1939; also London, Spring Books, 1964

David Garnett (editor), *The Essential T. E. Lawrence*, London, Jonathan Cape, 1951; New York, Dutton, 1952; Oxford, Oxford University Press, 1992

Malcolm Brown (editor), *The Letters of T. E. Lawrence*, London, Dent, 1988; Oxford, Oxford University Press, 1991: as *T. E. Lawrence: The Selected Letters*, New York, Norton, 1989; New York, Paragon Press, 1991

Richard Aldington, *Lawrence of Arabia: A Biographical Inquiry*, second edition, with introduction by Christopher Sykes, London, Collins, 1969

Philip Knightley & Colin Simpson, *The Secret Lives of Lawrence of Arabia*, London, Nelson, 1969; New York, McGraw Hill, 1970

John E. Mack, *A Prince of our Disorder: The Life of T. E. Lawrence*, London, Weidenfeld & Nicolson; Boston, Little, Brown, 1976; Oxford, Oxford University Press, 1991; Cambridge, Mass., Harvard Paperback 1998

H. Montgomery Hyde, *Solitary in the Ranks: T. E. Lawrence as Airman and Private Soldier*, London, Constable, 1977; New York, Atheneum, 1978

Stephen E. Tabachnick (editor), *The T. E. Lawrence Puzzle*, Athens, GA, University of Georgia Press, 1984

Stephen E. Tabachnick & Christopher Matheson, *Images of Lawrence*, London, Jonathan Cape, 1988

Jeremy Wilson, *Lawrence of Arabia: The Authorised Biography*, London, Heinemann, 1989, Minerva, 1990; New York, Atheneum, 1990

On Lawrence and modern warfare:
Robert Asprey, *War in the Shadows: The Guerrilla in History*, New York, Doubleday, 1975; London, MacDonald and Jane's, 1976.

Ian F. W. Beckett, *Modern Insurgencies and Counter-Insurgencies*, London and New York, Routledge, 2002

Research publication:
The Journal of the T. E. Lawrence Society, 1991– (P.O. Box 728, Oxford OX2 6YP) www.telsociety.org

Acknowledgments

In a book of this nature (and, I think I can say, of such obvious quality), the author is inevitably just one member of a team. Thus I can state without fear of contradiction that it would not be what it is without the crucial and imaginative contributions of its outstanding designer Nigel Soper and those members of the staff of Thames & Hudson who put so much effort and commitment into its creation. This book, however, is the product of a collaboration between the publishers and the Imperial War Museum, having been conceived as the companion volume to the Museum's exhibition on T. E. Lawrence mounted to coincide with the seventieth anniversary of his death in 1935. In this context I offer my special gratitude to the exhibition's curators, Angela Godwin, whose insights and ideas have greatly enriched this volume both in concept and content, and her colleague Penny Ritchie Calder, while simultaneously thanking Elizabeth Bowers, and Gemma Maclagan, of the Museum's Publications Office for their professional help in bringing the project to a satisfactory conclusion.

With regard to the vital matter of quotations from Lawrence's writings I am pleased to express my gratitude to the Seven Pillars of Wisdom Trust for granting the necessary permissions. For extracts from his wartime despatches, our joint thanks go to the National Archives (formerly the Public Record Office) at Kew. Additionally as author I wish to thank the executors of the war artist James McBey for permission to quote from a letter to Lowell Thomas written in 1962.

A number of highly valued friends have helped me directly with the making of this book. Thus I should like to record my great gratitude to Jack Flavell, Peter Metcalfe, Jeremy Wilson, Kathi Frances McGraw, Shea Johnson and Gigi Horsfield. I am also, as ever, deeply grateful to my wife Betty for her scrupulous scrutiny of my text (in its numerous, ever-changing versions) and her invaluable help in reading and correcting the proofs.

List of Illustrations

Dimensions of works are given in centimetres then inches, height before width.
Key: IWM = Imperial War Museum, a = above, b = below, c = centre, l = left, r = right.

Page

1 Augustus John, *T. E. Lawrence*, 1919. Pencil, 35.6 x 25.4 (14 x 10). National Portrait Gallery, London 3187

2–3 James McBey, *The Camel Corps: A Night March to Beersheba*, 1917. Black chalk, watercolour on paper. IWM ART 2926

6 T. E. Lawrence in Arab dress, 1919. Photograph by Harry Chase. IWM Q73535

10 Sarah Lawrence with four of her sons at Langley Lodge. Photograph possibly by Lawrence's father, *c.* 1895. Bodleian Library, Oxford

12a South Hill in Delvin, County Westmeath. Photograph

12b T. E. Lawrence's birthplace, Woodlands, Tremadoc, Wales. Photograph Gwynedd Archives

13 T. E. Lawrence aged three, *c.* 1891. Photograph

14 The four eldest Lawrence brothers in 1893: Montagu Robert, William George, Thomas Edward, Frank Helier. Photograph

15a & b The Lawrences' house in Oxford, 2 Polstead Road. Photograph. Malcolm Brown collection

16 City of Oxford High School for Boys. Photograph by Malcolm Brown

17a School register showing entries for Lawrence and his elder brother. Malcolm Brown collection

17b Oxford register. Malcolm Brown collection

18l Lawrence at City High School. Photograph. Oxford County Libraries

18r Brass rubbing of Thomas, Lord Berkeley from Wootton-under-Edge, Gloucestershire, by Lawrence. Ashmolean Museum, Oxford

19 Lawrence's bungalow at the bottom of the garden at Polstead Road, Oxford. Malcolm Brown collection

20a Jesus College, Oxford. Photograph by Malcolm Brown

20b Pen and ink sketch of Sahyun by Lawrence. Courtesy Seven Pillars of Wisdom Trust

21l Château Gaillard. Photograph and sketch by Lawrence. British Library, London

21r Sketch of Château Gaillard by Lawrence. Courtesy Seven Pillars of Wisdom Trust

22a 15th-century beaker excavated in Oxford. Ashmolean Museum, Oxford

22b 14th-century Baluster jug excavated in Oxford. Ashmolean Museum, Oxford

23l & r Watercolour illustrations of pottery found at Carchemish by Reginald Thompson with notes by Lawrence, 1911. British Museum, London

23b Lawrence's drawing of the inscriptions on the Yusuf Beg stone. Expedition notebook from Carchemish, 1911. British Museum, London

24 Lawrence in Dahoum's clothes, 1912. Photograph by Dahoum. British Library, London

25 Dahoum, 1912. Photograph by Lawrence. British Library, London. Courtesy Seven Pillars of Wisdom Trust

26 Carved lintel at Carchemish made by Lawrence in 1912. Haj Wahid standing in doorway. Photograph. British Museum, London. Courtesy Seven Pillars of Wisdom Trust

27a Archaeological camera Lawrence had specially made for himself in late 1910. Museum of the History of Science, Oxford

27b Lt Col. Stewart Newcombe and camel, March 1917. Photograph by Lawrence. IWM Q58908

28 Lawrence, Leonard Woolley and workers at Carchemish, 1913. Photograph. British Museum, London

29 Lawrence and Woolley, 1913. Photograph by Heinrich Franke. IWM Q73536

30l Fareedeh el Akle, 1921. Photograph. Courtesy the Beaumonts

30r Relief constructed from pieces found in excavations; Dahoum on left. Photograph by Lawrence. Bodleian Library, Oxford. Courtesy Seven Pillars of Wisdom Trust

31 Petra. Photograph by John Goodyer

32 David Bomberg, *Bab-Es-Siq, Petra*, 1924. Oil on canvas, 51.4 x 60.9 (20¼ x 24). Birmingham Museums and Art Gallery. © the Artist's Family/ Bridgeman Art Library

34 Lawrence at Akaba, 1917. Photograph. IWM Q59314

36 The Lawrence brothers, 1910. From left to right: T. E., Frank, Arnold, Bob and Will. Photograph. Private collection

37 Lawrence at British Headquarters in Cairo, 1 January 1917. Photograph. Hulton Archive/ Getty Images

38 Grand Sherif Hussein, Emir of Mecca, 12 December 1916. Photograph by the Staff Surgeon of H.M.S. Dufferin. IWM Q59888

40 Eric Kennington, *Emir Abdullah*, 1921. Chromo-lithograph, 24.4 x 18.5 (9⅝ x 7¼). Courtesy Seven Pillars of Wisdom Trust. © Family of the Artist

41 Augustus John, *Emir Feisal*, 1919. Oil on canvas, 72 x 53 (28⅜ x 20⅞). Ashmolean Museum, Oxford. © courtesy of the estate of Augustus John/Bridgeman Art Library

42 Lawrence in Arab dress, 1917. Photograph. IWM Q58817

43 James McBey, *Bodyguard to Emir Sherif Feisal*, 1918. Pencil and watercolour, 48.2 x 36.2 (19 x 14¼). IWM 1567

44l Quay at Yenbo, 1916. Photograph by Lawrence. IWM Q58728

44r House occupied by Lawrence in Yenbo, 1916–17. Photograph by Lawrence. IWM Q58821

46 Auda Abu Tayi, 1921. Photograph by Lawrence. Bodleian Library, Oxford. Courtesy Seven Pillars of Wisdom Trust

47 Eric Kennington, *Auda Abu Tayi*, 1921. Chromo-lithograph, 25 x 18.5 (9⅞ x 7¼). Courtesy Seven Pillars of Wisdom Trust. © Family of the Artist

48 Auda ibn Zaal, Mohammed Abu Tayi, an unknown Howeitat man, Auda Abu Tayi, Zaal ibn Motlog, 1921. Photograph by Lawrence. IWM Q60169

49 Colonel Pierce Joyce, Feisal and Jaafar Pasha in Wadi Kuntilla, August 1917. Photograph. IWM Q59011

51 Tulip bomb exploding on the railway line near Deraa. Photograph. IWM Q60020

52 Eric Kennington, *Lawrence*. Pastel. Courtesy Seven Pillars of Wisdom Trust. © Family of the Artist

54 Eric Kennington, *T. E. Lawrence*, 1921. Pastel. 44.7 x 32.8 (17⅝ x 12⅞). © Family of the Artist

56–57 Feisal's army entering Yenbo, December 1916. Photograph by Lawrence. IWM Q58754

59 Lowell Thomas's lantern slide of Jidda from the sea. Photograph by Harry Chase. © Lowell Thomas 2005

60 Jidda, 1921. Photograph by Lawrence. Courtesy Seven Pillars of Wisdom Trust

61 Jidda, 1921. Photograph by Lawrence. Courtesy Seven Pillars of Wisdom Trust

63 Emir Feisal at Wejh, March 1917. Photograph by Macrury. IWM Q58877

64–65 Camp at Nakhl Mubarak at dawn, December 1916. Photograph. IWM Q58838

66–67 Feisal's army on the first stage of the march to Wejh, 3 January 1917. Photograph by Lawrence. IWM Q58863

68–69 Feisal's army coming into Wejh, 25 January 1917. Photograph by Lawrence. IWM Q58841

70 inset Lawrence at Wejh, 1917. Photograph. IWM Q60912

70–71 Arab camp at Wejh, 1917. Photograph. IWM Q58811

72 Eric Kennington, *Sherif Ali ibn el Hussein*, 1921. Pastel, 76.2 x 50.8 (30 x 20). © Reading Museum Service (Reading Borough Council). All rights reserved

73 Sherif Sharref and troops on the march. Bir el Amri, March 1917. Photograph. IWM Q58939

74 Lawrence's 'shopping list' for supplies during the desert campaign, July 1917. British Library, London

75l Lawrence at Rabegh, north of Jidda, March 1917. Photograph. IWM Q60214

75r Lawrence at Akaba, 1917. Photograph. IWM Q60212

76 Main supply depot at Akaba, 1917. Photograph by Captain Goslett. IWM Q59548

77 The triumphal entry into Akaba, 6 July 1917. Photograph by Lawrence. IWM Q59193

78a James McBey, *General Sir Edmund Allenby, KCB*, 1918. Oil on canvas, 83.8 x 65.4 (33 x 25¾). IWM ART 1553

78b Emir Zeid's army arriving at Akaba, August 1917. Photograph by Captain Goslett. IWM Q59308

79 HMS *Humber* at Akaba. Photograph. IWM Q59064

80 & 81 Letter dated 11 August 1920 from Lawrence, with his diagram of the Akaba campaign, to Leonard Gotch. Collection Paul Gotch, Anthea Barker and Christopher Gotch

82–83 Unidentified desert scene. Photograph by Lawrence. IWM Q58933

84–85 Wadi Rumm. Photograph by Lawrence. IWM Q59363

86 Jebel el Sukhur. Photograph by Lawrence. IWM Q58957

87 Wadi Rumm. Photograph by Malcolm Brown

88–89 William Roberts, *Camel March*, 1923. Pen, ink and watercolour, 33 x 57 (13 x 22½). Courtesy Seven Pillars of Wisdom Trust. Estate of John David Roberts. Reproduced by permission of the William Roberts Society

90–91 Train on the Hejaz railway. Photograph. IWM Q59650

92 Hejaz railway at Abu Taka. Photograph. IWM Q59684

93 Wrecked train at Hadiya from the Arab campaign, 1968. Photograph by Hugh Leach

94–95 Ruins near Ma'an. Photograph probably by Lawrence. IWM Q60028

95 Turkish soldiers repairing the railway track near Maan. Photograph probably by Lawrence. IWM Q60116

96–97 Captain Wood, Thorne and Colonel Lawrence, 1917. Photograph. IWM Q60099

97l & r Lawrence's rifle given to him by Feisal. Photograph. IWM FIR 8255

98 Castle at Azrak. Photograph by Lawrence. IWM Q60022

99 Room where Lawrence slept in Azrak, November 1917. Photograph by Lawrence. IWM 60123

100 Lawrence by wrecked train. Photograph. Humanities Research Center Library, University of Texas at Austin

101 Yarmuk Valley bridge. Photograph. IWM Q59641

102 Jerusalem, December 1917. General Burton, followed by his two aides-de-camp, and Col. de Piepape, General Allenby and Lt Col. D'Agostino. Photograph. IWM Q12616

103 General Allenby's entry into Jerusalem, December 1917. Photograph. IWM Q1304

104–105 Henry Lamb, *Irish Troops in the Judean Hills Surprised by a Turkish Bombardment*, 1919. Oil on canvas, 182.9 x 218.4 (72 x 86). IWM ART 2746

106–107 Emir Zeid with Austrian guns captured at Tafileh, January 1918. Photograph. IWM Q59368

108–109 Lawrence with his bodyguard, Akaba, summer 1918. Photograph by Captain Goslett. IWM Q59576

110 Eric Kennington, *Mahmas ibn Dakhil*, 1921. Chromo-lithograph, 25 x 18.5 (9⅞ x 7¼). Courtesy Seven Pillars of Wisdom Trust. © Family of the Artist

111 Eric Kennington, *Muttar il Hamoud Min Bini Hassan*, 1920. Pastel, 76.8 x 55.9 (30¼ x 22). © Tate, London 2005

112 Armoured Rolls Royce. Photograph. IWM Q59376

113 Talbot car in Wadi Itm: Auda, Hejris, Mirzuk, Feisal, late March 1918. Photograph by Harry Chase. IWM Q60048

114a Biplanes of the Royal Flying Corps. IWM Q59035

114b An Arab inspecting the machine-gun of a Bristol F.2B biplane. IWM Q58702

Index